CLASSIC QUILTS

from

THE AMERICAN MUSEUM IN BRITAIN

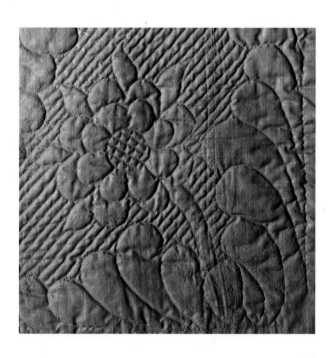

D1438546

CLAILTS

THE AM BRITAIN

Presented to
2nd Air Division Memorial Library
Trust Collection
In memory of those Americans
who, flying from bases in these parts,
gave their lives defending freedom

1942 - 1945

LAURA BERESFORD and KATHERINE HEBERT
Curators, The American Museum in Britain

SCALA

Foreword

The American Museum in Britain is fortunate to have a superior collection of quilts, many of which are on display. These pieces not only demonstrate the skill and patience of their creators but are also historical objects of their era, and each reflects its own time. Often there is some commentary, one not written in words but shown in symbols and subtleties. Some of the quilts reflect the politics of their periods, such as those featuring famous people: President Harrison and the Marquis de Lafayette.

Others reflect in more subtle ways issues such as slavery or religious beliefs. These fine artistic works have much to tell us, if we look closely and with an open mind. Of course, we enjoy them for their beauty, but the story behind the aesthetic will lead us to their history and cultural context and inform the story of America.

Sandra Barghini, Director
The American Museum in Britain

HALF-TITLE: Pink Whole-Cloth Quilt, detail (see pp.20–1).

FRONTISPIECE: Lady Liberty holding the Union flag from Album Quilt Top, detail (see pp.44–5).

TITLE PAGE: Rose of Sharon Quilt, detail (see pp.34–5).

LEFT: Tippecanoe and Tyler Too Quilt, detail (see pp.60–1).

RIGHT: Star of Bethlehem Quilt, detail (see pp.78–9).

Preface by Shiela Betterton

The quilt and coverlet collection of The American Museum in Britain is considered to be the finest in Europe and ranks high with those in the United States as well. For thirty years, it was my privilege to care for this world-renowned collection after I was appointed textiles and needlework specialist for the museum in 1974. I had come to the museum as a guide in 1963, when the museum's quilts numbered about sixty. I was intrigued as to why American quilts should have the same quilting patterns as those under which I slept as a child in Northumberland. So started my researches – long before the great quilt revival of the 1970s.

A true quilt is a textile sandwich, with a top layer of fabric, a bottom layer and a filling for warmth in between. The top may be plain fabric, patchwork, appliqué or a combination of techniques. Quilting is the pattern in running stitch that holds the layers together and is the last process in the making of a quilt.

The technique of quilting has been known for hundreds of years. It originated in the East and then travelled through the Middle East and thence across Europe to Britain and eventually to North America. Early European quilts were purely utilitarian, the stitching being the minimal required to hold the three layers in place. In medieval times quilted jackets were worn under metal armours to prevent chafing, and light troops had only a quilted jacket for protection. However, it was soon recognized that quilting could be decorative, and during the eighteenth century clothing was quilted for warmth: men wore quilted breeches and waistcoats, and women quilted petticoats and bodices.

Women from Britain and parts of Europe took with them to America their knowledge of quilting. Until the time of the American Revolution, therefore, American and British 'best' quilts were very similar. When America was a colony, the mother country did little to encourage textile manufacture and, despite the very early establishment of a textile factory at Rowley, Massachusetts, weaving remained largely a cottage industry until the late eighteenth century. Deprived of facilities to manufacture their own textiles, the American colonists had to import from Europe and the East by way of Britain. Fabrics such as ginghams, dimity and damask, together with Indian chintzes and calicoes imported by the British East India Company, began to be available in America.

LEFT: Shiela Betterton with a Grandmother's Flower Garden quilt, June 1976.

OPPOSITE: Square-in-a-Square Quilt, detail (see pp.102–3).

Many of the early textiles were blue-dyed, possibly because indigo is a reliable dye, fast and strong enough to cover small discolorations and imperfections in the cloth. Until about 1750, textiles were printed in black, reds, purples and browns – all derived from madder. However, the 'Turkey red' dye, long known in the East and the first permanent red dye, was introduced into America in about 1829. From then on, there was a proliferation of red and white quilts, often with green added.

It is a tradition that an American girl should have up to twelve quilts in her 'hope chest', or possibly thirteen – the thirteenth being her Bride's quilt. She began to piece the tops at an early age but, as a general rule, these were not backed and quilted until she became engaged. One superstition warned that any girl who made a quilt on her own would die unmarried. Bridal chest quilts were usually finished by friends and family.

The majority of quilts would be made at home by the mother and her daughters. Others were quilted at a 'quilting bee' or 'quilting', which was a welcome social occasion, particularly in the lives of pioneer women who lived far apart. Many quilting bees lasted a whole day. The largest room in the house was cleared, and one or more quilting frames might be set up. If there was not room in the house, the frames could be put up in the barn. The women would bring lunch with them and those who were not quilting took turns in the

kitchen. Good needlewomen were always sought after and those whose sewing was not up to standard threaded needles and helped generally. When their work for the day was done, the men joined the party. The quilt frames were put away and the hostess provided as grand a supper as she was able. After the meal there were usually games, music and dancing.

Patterns for the pieced and appliqué tops were taken from everyday objects. Women looked at the flowers and foliage around their homes – or even the houses themselves – and could see in them the making of an attractive design. Historical events also gave names to patterns. Queen Charlotte's Crown, for instance, refers to the last queen the colonies had before becoming the United States of America. Quilting patterns likewise covered a wide range. Household items such as thimbles, cups, dinner plates and even flat irons were used as a basis of quilting designs. Some had meanings: the pineapple was a symbol of hospitality, for example, the pomegranate, of fruitfulness, and grapes, of plenty.

Fifty years ago, little was known in Britain about American quilts, so the founders of The American Museum in Britain decided to make quilts a feature of their museum. Such is the regard in which the American Museum's quilt collection is held that many prized examples have been donated to the museum to be enjoyed by a wider public. Over the years, the quilt collection has become so important that several illustrated catalogues have been produced. This volume is the latest in this series – lavishly illustrated, with a revised and up-to-date text – which will be welcomed by all lovers of this art form.

Shiela Betterton
December 2008

Shiela Betterton – herself one of the treasures of The American Museum in Britain – passed away on Boxing Day 2008. Shiela first worked at the museum as a volunteer guide in the 1960s and continued to steward after her retirement as the museum's textiles and needlework specialist in 1994. She was inducted into the American Quilters' Hall of Fame in 1999.

This book is dedicated to our friend Shiela, as well as to Dr Dallas Pratt and John Judkyn, the founders of The American Museum in Britain.

The Making of The American Museum in Britain and its Quilt Collection

The American Museum in Britain, based at Claverton Manor in Bath, opened to the public in July 1961 – the long-cherished project of its founders, Dr Dallas Pratt (an American psychiatrist and collector) and John Judkyn (a British-born antiques dealer who had become a United States citizen in 1954).

The intention behind the making of the museum was to showcase American decorative arts in Britain, thereby creating a better understanding of the history of the United States and its people among British visitors, whose conception of both was largely dictated by gun-slinging stereotypes popularized in Hollywood films. Moreover, the stock character of the American cultural bumpkin had often featured in British writing since the 'invasion' of the aristocracy by the so-called 'dollar princesses' in the late nineteenth century. Despite evidence to the contrary, this caricature proved tenacious – especially after the additional 'invasion' of American servicemen during the Second World War and their ongoing presence in the economically bleak years that followed.

Fifty years hence, it is difficult to understand how enormously different the world was in the mid-twentieth century. Cold War animosities were entrenched – necessitating the ongoing presence of American servicemen in Britain – and the nuclear threat was ubiquitous. Russian overtures in Cuba were already beginning to trouble Washington in the summer of 1961, as hosts and guests celebrated the opening of The American Museum in Britain and, by extension, the special relationship that existed between the United Kingdom and the United States.

At the core of the making of the museum was another transatlantic alliance: that between Dallas Pratt (1914–1994) and John Judkyn (1913–1963), who had met in 1937. Within days of their initial encounter, they had begun their emotional and intellectual partnership, which was to endure for over two decades. They were discreet about their relationship, even within their families. Much to his later amusement, for instance, young Dallas had not been allowed to go to Oxford because his then step-father thought it unsuitable for the boy as the university was full of 'perverts', unlike Cambridge. Their continuing subterfuge, once they had come together as a couple, was so successful that one of Judkyn's female relations even mused, briefly, about her chance of becoming Mrs Pratt.

Dallas had long before concluded that his mother, Beatrice, had been sufficient 'Mrs Pratt' for the world to digest and did not see the point of ever creating another. A favourite grandchild of the Standard Oil magnate Henry Huttleston Rogers, Beatrice inherited $6 million (the equivalent of several billion in current figures) on the death of 'Hell Hound' (as her grandfather was known on Wall Street). Beatrice, 'the most fashionably dressed married woman of the exclusive set', according to an anonymous Newport reporter in 1918, did none the less manage to exhaust a great deal of this massive wealth on herself. Another columnist at this time gushed with perhaps unintentional irony:

[A]s an outlet for her temperament Mrs Pratt decided to express herself fully in her town house. She took two old-fashioned brownstone houses on Upper Park Avenue, turned them into one, had the whole outside painted a gleaming white and did her front door with several coats of scarlet lacquer!

If the outside of the house made New York start, the inside made them gasp. Everything that was not scarlet or bright sky blue was black. And the last exotic touches were given by flocks of parrots, parakeets and cockatoos that had the run of the house. The effect was stupefying but not conducive to a tranquil domestic life.[1]

Public knowledge of her spending extravaganzas, such as that described above, provoked considerable mirth in American society pages in 1918, when Beatrice sued Aleck Pratt – the first of her four husbands – for divorce, citing non-support. She also complained that her husband had, in effect, deserted her by entering military service. Newspaper society columnists in Newport, New York and Washington were delighted to have such an opportunity to comment publicly while remaining anonymous (thus protecting their places in the 'exclusive set'):

*She and Aleck have led dogs' lives for two or three years, only happy
when separated. Each one trying determinedly to make the other as
uncomfortable as possible. At the time Aleck enlisted he said that no
matter how frightful the war might be anything was better than living
with Pugsey. His pet name for the stately Beatrice.*

Beatrice's divorce petition was granted in just nine minutes, with her
gaining complete custody of her children. The ruling was much to the
satisfaction of 'The Club Fellow' in the *Washington Mirror*, who
attested that Beatrice was 'in every way a most devoted mother' – an
opinion not echoed by her children, who had learned even by this
tender age to turn to their nanny (nicknamed 'Dear') for maternal
love. Reviewing his early childhood in later years, Dr Pratt wrote :

*My desolate afternoons at school, when I wandered around alone and
felt lonely and dejected. I have disliked the afternoons ever since.*
    *The final rejection is by Mamma. It was not Dear who preferred her
to Daddy, it was I as a small child. But she rejected me.*[2]

Ironically, it is due to the wealth of 'dearest Mamma' that the making
of The American Museum in Britain was accomplished. Beatrice died
in 1956, and each of her children received part of what remained of
her fortune.

With this boon came a period of reflection. In 1942, Pratt had
qualified as a psychiatrist and served in overcrowded and under-
staffed army hospitals in conditions that were often distressing to
both patients and physicians.[3] He was later sent to the Pacific. In the
post-war years, Dr Pratt practised at Columbia University's medical
centre. His work continued to interest him, but he wondered whether

Judkyn remained as satisfied in his own lucrative business endeavours,
importing antique English furniture into America, and in his posts
on various committees (including the New York Board of the English-
Speaking Union). Was he making the most of his talents?

As a Quaker, Judkyn had successfully applied to be registered as a
conscientious objector on both sides of the Atlantic during the war.
(He had resided in the United States with Pratt, since 1937.) In his
British application Judkyn nevertheless acknowledged:

*[M]y responsibilities as a British Citizen are most important, and
when my country is at war I cannot take a purely negative attitude, on
the ground that I am against war and will have no part in it. I recognize
that I am as much to blame for what has come about as many others
and am as anxious to achieve the same ends as most of my fellow
countrymen [...]*[4]

Consequently, Judkyn spent the war volunteering for the Friends
Relief Service; in the last years of the fighting, he himself supervised
the distribution of food and medicine donated by American Quakers
to civilian victims in London and France. Judkyn had been anxious to
work towards the bettering of Anglo-American relations since his
arrival in the United States in 1937. Writing in 1946, he reiterated this
concern after witnessing the devastation in Europe:

*I feel that [...] the promotion of deeper understanding and fellowship
between England and the US is absolutely basic to any sort of world
peace in the future.*[5]

Judkyn was disheartened by the misunderstandings that continued
on both sides of the Atlantic, despite the camaraderie fostered in the
war years. From his own personal experience, he appreciated that
prejudices are old habits and die hard.

Spurred on by these money matters and meditations in 1956,
Dr Pratt and John Judkyn thus began to entertain the possibility of
establishing a museum of Americana in Britain that would challenge
preconceptions about the cultural inheritance of the United States.
The idea had arisen after they had toured several American historic
house and 'living history' museums. These attractions included
Historic Deerfield and Old Sturbridge Village (Massachusetts),

Colonial Williamsburg (Virginia) and the Henry Francis du Pont Winterthur Museum (Delaware) – the last created by their friend 'Harry' du Pont at his family home. Dr Pratt later recalled:

It struck me as very odd that [...] not a single collection, much less a museum, of American cultural-historic artefacts existed outside of the United States [...] At this stage, my desire was simply to share with the British the aesthetic charm of early American furniture and decorative arts and their historical background. John added a concern of his own: to inform the British [...] of the outstanding American achievements in these arts and crafts, a subject about which he believed them to be woefully ignorant.[6]

Collecting for the museum began in earnest in 1958, facilitated by Judkyn's business contacts – each piece testifying to the artistry of Americans and how they had lived in the past. Buying expeditions across the United States had to be accommodated within small pockets of 'free' time in between work commitments. Since scarcely any time was indeed 'free' for either Pratt or Judkyn, these excursions were aggressively scheduled, with little more than a day in each destination. Dr Pratt later observed that he and Judkyn were not the only ones physically and mentally exhausted by this 'whirlwind collecting'[7]:

[O]rganizing a trip like this, in the days before computers, was a task almost beyond the power of the railways (we travelled from New York to Colorado Springs, Santa Fé, El Paso, Mexico City, San Antonio, New Orleans, St Louis and back to New York). John Wilson, our young secretary, fresh out of England, made trip after trip to Pennsylvania Station, urging, demanding and begging that they produce the complete ticket before our departure date. He was so distraught that, as he admitted later, only when he actually broke down and wept at the ticket window did the clerk make a supreme effort and produce the many-sectioned tickets, each at least a yard long.[8]

Dr Pratt's notebooks from this period are filled with measurements and sketches. These rough drawings were often supplemented with photographs, since purchasing decisions could not always be made instantaneously, in case a better example might be unearthed elsewhere, 'or a more reasonably priced one'.[9]

The search was also under way for a suitable home for the museum. Initially, the two men considered locating their museum in London. Friends argued, however, that visitors to the capital did not want to tour museums: 'They wanted to buy a hat or see the Palladium show.'[10] It was eventually decided that the museum should be established in Bath, one of the finest architectural settings in Britain, only a few miles from Judkyn's British business base at Freshford Manor. Another deciding factor was the presence at Freshford of the furniture and paintings restorer C. A. (Nick) Bell Knight, whose business slogan was 'Nothing Too Intricate'.[11]

After a year of searching in the Bath area, a suitable home for The American Museum in Britain was discovered: Claverton Manor, an elegant bow-fronted, neo-classical house overlooking the idyllic Limpley Stoke valley. It had been built in 1820 by Jeffry Wyatt (later known as Sir Jeffry Wyatville, after refashioning St George's Hall at Windsor Castle for George IV). Given their interest in strengthening ties between the UK and the USA, the museum's founders were elated to learn that the home they had chosen for their venture was also where, in 1897, the great Anglo-American and future prime minister Winston Churchill made his début as a public speaker. Churchill's mother, Jennie Jerome, had been one of the most celebrated 'dollar princesses'. Thirty years later, Dr Pratt reminisced about the first time he saw the property:

Before seeing the interior of the house, we walked on the lawn [...] I turned around and saw the exquisite front façade of the manor [...] Before we had even entered the house, I knew our search was over.[12]

As well as furniture and furnishings, panelling and floors were also shipped over to Britain at the instigation of Pratt and Judkyn, enabling period rooms from demolished buildings in America to be reconstructed within the spacious interiors of Claverton Manor. It was Nick Bell Knight's task to make everything fit seamlessly, the New World cocooned within the Old. He subsequently recalled:

RIGHT: John Judkyn and
Dallas Pratt in the south
of France, late 1950s.

*My first impression was of endless corridors and passages […] The
interior had to be literally gutted to accommodate the reconstructions of
period rooms. The vast pile of timbers and miscellany presented a colossal
nightmarish jigsaw puzzle. I used to dream that I was condemned until
eternity to sort out dentils and pilasters, feather-edging and sills each into
their respective piles, whilst little imps mixed them all up again.*[13]

The museum project vied for attention with various teaching and
business commitments in America, prompting Judkyn and Pratt to
zigzag the Atlantic while Bell Knight stayed at Claverton, working so
hard that he drove himself to the point of collapse in early 1961.[14]
Still, he had worked wonders, as Dr Pratt discovered on returning to
Britain in May to prepare for the museum's opening:

*I had one of the greatest moments of my life on entering the Museum.
It was virtually finished […] Everything we had dreamed 3,000 miles
away had materialized in the improbable setting of an English manor on
a Somerset hillside. And the ultimate sensation was this. Not only did the
historical rooms look exactly like those in the American houses I had seen
and stayed in over the years. You could close your eyes and the experience
of being in America not only persisted, it increased, because the old
panelling and beams had brought the* <u>*scent*</u> *of America with them.*[15]

Since its opening almost fifty years ago, one of the most popular
attractions at The American Museum in Britain has been the Textile
Room, a purpose-built exhibition space rather than a recreated
historic interior (although many quilts are also showcased in the
period room settings elsewhere in the museum). Nearly fifty quilts are
on view in the Textile Room at any one time, and almost half of these
are rotated annually, so that interested visitors can keep returning to
see more of the museum's extensive collection – the most significant
of its type outside the United States and the equal of many premier
collections across the Atlantic.

The museum has over two hundred quilt masterworks, most of
them American. These abstract expanses of colour, texture and
design appeal to an audience increasingly familiar with conceptual
experimentations in painting. Traditionally, quilts have been more
often valued as historic artefacts than as works of art: decorative but
functional examples of domestic craft prompted by necessity (the
pervasive idea of hand-stitched scraps cobbled together to provide
warmth, a myth that lingers even now). The re-evaluation of quilts
as expressions of creative energy began in the United States when
collectors of contemporary work began buying American folk art
from the eighteenth and nineteenth centuries. These pieces often
featured silhouettes of flat colour and bold design – elements in
common with modern art.

In May 1958, John Judkyn presented an exhibition of quilts at his
English home, Freshford Manor. Dr Pratt later acknowledged that
this undertaking (to raise funds for the village church) was 'one of
the germs of the concept of an American museum in Bath'.[16]
The exhibition consisted of fine examples of quilts and quilting
dating from 1650 to 1850, selected from various private and public
collections on both sides of the Atlantic. Judkyn himself had chosen
the quilts on view (some from his own personal collection). Where
possible, the quilts were displayed in rooms furnished with antiques
appropriate to their period – such as carved tester beds ('themselves
of great interest'[17]). Star pieces included an English quilt made from
over a thousand snippets of pink and grey silk and an Album quilt of
seventy-two blocks loaned from the Shelburne Museum in Vermont,
signed by those who had helped to stitch the squares – men as well as
women, to the delighted surprise of visitors to the Freshford show.

It was after visiting the Shelburne Museum – created by the eclectic
folk art collector Electra Havemeyer Webb – that Judkyn and Pratt
fully appreciated how important a gallery display of textiles would be
to their museum's success in promoting American decorative arts.
Quilts from the United States had not been widely seen in Britain.

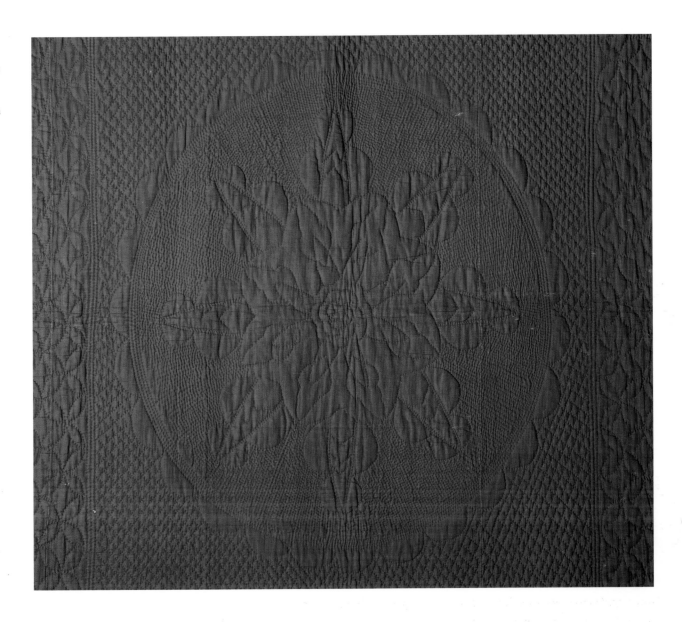

Indeed the Freshford exhibition was one of the first opportunities to view this American vernacular art form in abundance. As well as loaning pieces to the Freshford show, Mrs Webb also helped Judkyn and Pratt form the nucleus of the quilt collection of The American Museum in Britain. Dr Pratt later described a memorable excursion undertaken at Mrs Webb's suggestion:

Mrs Webb was kind enough to give us the name of one of her principal suppliers of quilts. We lost no time driving to Ephrata, Pennsylvania, but sped straight past the shop on the main street which, although it bore a small sign reading 'Antiques', also displayed candy and inexpensive trinkets in the shop window. However, this proved in fact to be the precious depository known to Mrs Webb. Presiding over the candy and the souvenirs was Mrs Spangler, an old lady of Pennsylvania Dutch background [...] She invited us upstairs to see 'what I have in the bedroom'. What she had was all piled on one bed, a mountain of quilts. One by one, John and I peeled them off [...] [W]e bought twelve coverlets [...] Alas, since Mrs Spangler died not long afterwards, it was the last collection which could be assembled from sources to which only she had access.[18]

This 'treasures in the attic' experience is the kind that museum curators long to live themselves and serves as a reminder of how fortuitous it was that Pratt and Judkyn embarked on their museum enterprise when they did. A few years later, it would not have been possible for them to gather so comprehensive a collection of Americana – let alone such a pre-eminent collection of American quilts.

Some of the first quilts acquired for the collection are also the earliest: glazed worsted Whole-Cloth quilts – bed coverings from the late eighteenth century, when the United States came into being.[19] The early colonists had brought Whole-Cloth quilts with them to begin life in the New World. Imported quilts are itemized luxuries in wills and inventories from the early seventeenth century. As well as providing physical heat, these bedcovers would have given emotional comfort to settlers, who could still have wrapped themselves, metaphorically, in the warmth of loved ones left behind across the sea.

The textile industry was slow to develop in America. With a Whole-Cloth quilt sewn over a hundred years later than those brought over

LEFT: Cut-out chintz block from an Album quilt with motifs similar to those seen on contemporary ceramics (see pp.44–5).

by Puritan settlers, the quilt top and backing would still have been made from lengths of brightly coloured fabric imported from England and France. A layer of padding was sandwiched between these for warmth – most often, sheep's wool. The three levels, which collectively form the quilt itself, were then held together by decorative lines of tight running stitch – the quilting – which gave sculptural form and linear shape to flowing designs of stylized flowers, hearts, fruit and other motifs linked with diagonal lines or cross-hatching.

Worried about the potential loss of their livelihood, British weavers successfully campaigned to have the domestic sale of printed cottons from India prohibited during the first decades of the eighteenth century. (The ban was not lifted until 1774.) Exports of these materials and the European printed fabrics they inspired, however, were still permissible. As a means of protecting this lucrative trade, skilled textile workers were often denied permission to emigrate to America from Britain. Technical innovations in copper-engraving from the mid-century meant that enormous quantities of printed chintzes were shipped across the Atlantic instead – an estimated

four million yards by 1800. Quilt-making conventions were reworked to accommodate this new material to best advantage.

Popular at the end of the eighteenth century, the appliqué technique was, in essence, an embellishment of the European Whole-Cloth tradition used in the preceding centuries. Decorative motifs reminiscent of those on painted porcelain plates (such as birds on the wing) or vibrantly coloured silhouettes were cut from lengths of imported chintz, their edges folded under to form a hem and then each printed fragment individually stitched onto a backing fabric. This formed the quilt top. Extra padding was sometimes slipped beneath the appliquéd decoration to give a more sculpted appearance. The quilting patterns often echoed the subjects of the applied decoration, thus unifying the disparate parts. As quilts became worn, the appliquéd printed features could be removed and re-stitched to another backing material.

Template pieced quilts or mosaic patchwork also evolved from similar matters of economy in the later eighteenth century. Using paper

templates, fabric fragments left over from other sewing tasks could be cut into uniform geometric shapes, such as diamonds and hexagons. Each segment of the mosaic would then be joined together with close running stitches. The papers are removed after the interlocking quilt top has been completed. Paper templates often remain in unfinished quilts – scraps of letters and scribbled accounts, another instance of the maker's handiwork. One of the most dramatic examples of this type of quilt in the collection of The American Museum in Britain is an expansive Tumbling Blocks pattern, pieced in a twelve-pointed star, which is almost nine feet square.[20] Its three-dimensional playfulness would have delighted the graphic artist M. C. Escher, whose drawings contain similar quirks of perception. A sunburst quilt – an explosion of pastel paisley diamonds – likewise dazzles with its technical lustre and painterly exuberance.[21]

Block piecing dominated American quilt-making from the mid-nineteenth century. While not necessarily an American development, the block quilt was none the less a composite method of quilt-making that would come to be recognized as indisputably 'American' – if only

as a style reference. As in mosaic quilt tops, the block quilt has a modular construction, with linked units sometimes juxtaposing decorative motifs with alternating blocks of solid colour. The pre-eminence of the block quilt in the nineteenth century was largely due to its convenience. Little space was needed for sewing individual blocks; the work, as a consequence, was less onerous and much more portable. Previously quilt-making had been confined to the home, with a communal celebration – or 'quilting' – occurring at the end of a solitary process, when friends and family came together to complete a quilt. Recognized as a social occasion, a quilting might end with festivities and a special supper.

Coinciding with the fashion for Album quilts in the mid-nineteenth century, the pieced block method enabled and encouraged wider participation in quilt construction. The decorated sections were often the collaborative achievement of several quilters, who contributed a block and could sign it, for posterity, as their personal work.

From 1840 black indelible ink was available, allowing quilters to pen onto fabric messages of friendship, snippets of poetry and favourite lines from the scriptures. The American Museum in Britain has many striking block quilts in its collection, notably an example from the Civil War period with inked precepts and a block featuring a determined Lady Liberty flourishing the Union flag.[22] Perhaps the greatest treasure of this type in the museum, however, is the vibrantly coloured and boldly executed Baltimore Album quilt, which stretches to over 10 feet square – a presentation piece of monumental proportions that bestows as much prestige on the signatories as it does on the (now forgotten) recipients.[23] These quilts were particularly popular in the prosperous Baltimore area, which lends its name to them.

As the nineteenth century progressed, other regional styles evolved. Visitors to the Textile Room at The American Museum in Britain are met with a kaleidoscopic assortment of many types of quilts from the

BELOW: Symmetrical appliquéd silhouettes of solid colour
framed by radiating bands of contour quilting are a distinct
Hawaiian quilt style. Detail from Hawaiian quilt, 1950–70
(1972.167).

United States, as diverse as the numerous ethnic communities that
none the less identify themselves as 'American'.[24] For the purposes of
reviewing the quilt collection at The American Museum in Britain,
the most significant of these idiosyncratic variations are the Amish
and Hawaiian quilt styles, which employ distinctive visual elements
and colour palettes.

The Amish – Anabaptists who took part in William Penn's trial of
religious tolerance in what became known as Pennsylvania – started
making quilts (usually pieced) in the mid-nineteenth century,
following more contact with their non-Amish neighbours.
Dominated by sober colour combinations and austere geometric
patterns, most surviving early Amish quilts date from after 1880.[25]
It was the age of the mass-produced treadle sewing machine – an
innovation the Amish were quick to adopt for use in their quilt-
making, despite their general resistance to new technologies.

The distinct Hawaiian quilt style – symmetrical appliquéd silhouettes
of expansive solid colour framed by radiating lines of contour
quilting – was also prompted by religious impulse, albeit on the part
of missionaries keen to curb the exuberance of the islanders under
their jurisdiction. Historically, the indigenous population used felted
and dyed cloth made from beaten mulberry bark for bedcovers.
Missionaries taught their female pupils quilting as a distraction from

cultural traditions that conflicted with Protestant perceptions of ladylike behaviour. The resulting quilts were a bold fusion of inherited decorative motifs with introduced techniques, tools and textiles.[26]

Given the warm climate of the Hawaiian islands, quilt-making was embraced there primarily as an unhampered creative opportunity for women otherwise constrained by social niceties. Another instance of this artistic liberation is the 'craze for Crazies' – the late nineteenth-century fervour for Crazy quilts, which replicated the asymmetrical fragmentation of Roman *tesserae* (the original 'crazy paving') and the cracklature in the over-glazing of oriental ceramics (then championed by devotees of the Aesthetic Movement as items essential to the interior decoration of one's home[27]). Made up from apparently random scraps of luxurious combinations of silks and velvets, Crazy quilts are more correctly decorative spreads: these textile treasures do not always have internal batting. Instead of warming beds, Crazy quilts were more often used as conversation pieces to drape over furniture. The materials were enhanced further with embroidery and embellishments. Specific scraps or pieces of applied decoration could represent significant moments and specific people. In one of the spectacular Crazy quilts in the American Museum's collection, for example, several generations of a family are personified by dress fabric remnants.[28]

Quilt designs began to appear in print as early as the 1830s, but it was not until the end of the nineteenth century that publishers fully appreciated the potential for this market and invested heavily in mail order patterns. Several quilts in the museum's collection originated as kits but have become 'originals' in their own right by the quilting proficiency of their makers.[29] Quilt-making in the United States declined in the early twentieth century until the economic hardships of the Great Depression of the 1930s renewed the pastime, as did the transatlantic relief schemes during the Second World War – one of the earliest appearances of the American quilt before the British public. Often distributed by the Red Cross to victims of bombed cities, these quilts became tangible symbols of the special relationship between the United States and the United Kingdom.[30]

It was partly this type of Anglo-American fellowship that inspired Dr Dallas Pratt and John Judkyn to establish The American Museum in Britain. As it approaches its fiftieth anniversary, these cultural ties

The sense of achievement in the success of the American Museum was undercut when Judkyn was killed in a car accident during the summer of 1963, just after his fiftieth birthday. In shock, Pratt wrote at the time:

I feel as if something of myself died […] but, if so, how am I able to eat and laugh and already for brief moments, forget? I have a great fear of forgetting – not in a gross sense, of course, but in the sense that time may begin to blur and obliterate that unique personality.[31]

remain paramount to all aspects of the museum. From its earliest days, praise of the museum has been considerable – especially for its superlative collection of American quilts and the manner of its display, with visitors essentially walking into the illustrated pages of a gigantic storybook (an arrangement used at the Shelburne Museum).

He need not have worried. As long as The American Museum in Britain continues – presenting to the British public the artistic heritage of the peoples of the United States – it stands as a memorial to these two extraordinary personalities and to their own enduring transatlantic alliance.

NOTES

1. All clippings quoted in this section were collected by Beatrice herself and pasted (often without reference to newspaper title) in scrapbooks now deposited in the archives of The American Museum in Britain.

2. Quoted in Dick Chapman, *Dallas Pratt: A Patchwork Biography* (Cambridge: Mark Argent, 2004), p.112. Beatrice was disconcerted when her eldest son, Dallas, published a slim volume of his poetry in 1931 and dedicated it to Dear (his 'beloved governess, Maud Duke'). Pratt took care that the dedicatee of his second poetry collection (published seven years later) was Beatrice. Still, he could not resist a wry comment: 'Dedicated to Mamma – *Madame Va et Vient*' (volumes in A.M.I.B. archives).

3. Dr Pratt described his work in one such institution in a letter (dated 28 March 1943, A.M.I.B. archives) to his mother from Valley Forge General Hospital, Phoenixville: 'I am working very hard. But it is like a mouse nibbling at a mountain. I have four wards and about 45 patients directly under my supervision. It is too many […] I am Jack of all Trades, and do everything from censoring letters to tieing [*sic*] disturbed patients down. This latter aspect of Psychiatry is one in which I am not at all interested, but comes under the heading of military duty, so must be done without grousing.'

4. British application, 22 January 1944 (A.M.I.B. archives).

5. Quoted in Chapman, *Dallas Pratt*, p.125.

6. Dr Pratt writing in July 1991 of John Judkyn and how they came to found the American Museum together (A.M.I.B. archives).

7. Dallas Pratt, 'Whirlwind Collecting', *America in Britain* (1965), pp.2–5.

8. Dallas Pratt writing in the early 1990s, notebook commentary 4/2 (A.M.I.B. archives).

9. Dallas Pratt, notebook commentary 8/1 (A.M.I.B. archives).

10. John Judkyn quoted in the *Bristol Evening World* (19 April 1961), p.3.

11. In a letter dated June 1961, Judkyn wrote to Bell Knight: 'If it had not been for the knowledge that you would be available, we would never have attempted the museum project.' C.A. Bell Knight papers (A.M.I.B. archives).

12. From Dr Pratt's speech delivered on the thirtieth anniversary of The American Museum in Britain in 1991 (A.M.I.B. archives).

13. C.A. Bell Knight papers (A.M.I.B. archives).

14. Years later, Bell Knight reflected (A.M.I.B. archives): '[F]or three years I was living "only" for the one thing – the creation of the American Museum. I poured every ounce of effort and skills into the enterprise. I became almost unbearable to live with … days were too short, nights were too long – if it was at all possible I would have worked 24 hours, seven days a week, but my constitution would not permit that […]'

15. Dallas Pratt, notebook commentary 10/2 (A.M.I.B. archives).

16. Dallas Pratt, 'Collecting Quilts' (A.M.I.B. archives).

17. As noted in the brochure promoting this event to a potential London audience (A.M.I.B. archives).

18. Dallas Pratt, 'Collecting Quilts' (A.M.I.B. archives).

19. 2004.22 and 1962.22. See pp.20–3

20. 1962.91. See pp.104–5

21. 1966.261. See pp.80–1.

22. 1959.167. See pp.44–5.

23. 1964.5. See pp.46–7.

24. 'America is not like a blanket – one piece of unbroken cloth, the same color, the same texture, the same size,' declared Jesse Jackson in 1984, 'America is more like a quilt – many patches, many pieces, many colors, many sizes, all woven and held together by a common thread.' ('The Rainbow Coalition', speech delivered to the Democratic Party, 17 July 1984.)

25. 1977.93 and 1977.2 are outstanding examples of this distinct Amish style. See pp.108, 110–11.

26. 1972.157 and 1972.161. See pp.116–19.

27. Along with Japanese fans, a motif often embroidered on Crazy quilts from both sides of the Atlantic. The American-born artist James Abbott McNeill Whistler was a leading aesthete in London, along with his rival in wit Oscar Wilde. The latter toured America in 1882, lecturing on 'The House Beautiful'.

28. 1980.68. See pp.88–9.

29. 1998.156 and 1997.110. See pp.70–1, 76–7.

30. 2000.10 and 1998.123. See pp.122–3.

31. Letter dated 1 August 1963 (A.M.I.B. archives) to David Johnson, the museum's first Assistant Director.

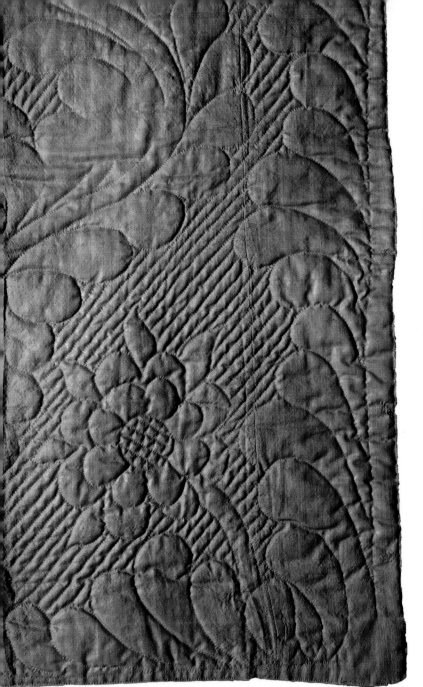

Notes

A glossary of quilting terms is on page 126.

In the dimensions given for all quilts, length precedes width.

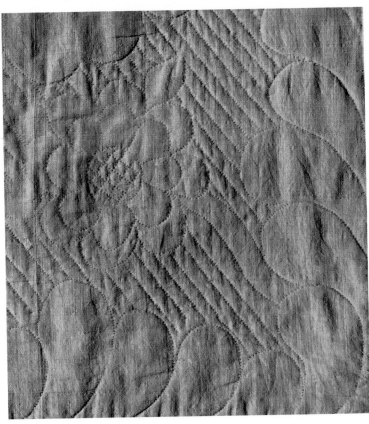

LEFT: Running feather vine and English rose quilting.

ABOVE: Unglazed khaki-coloured wool backs the quilt.

Pink Whole-Cloth Quilt

1760–80
Eastern Seaboard, America
269 x 213 cm (106 x 84 in)
2004.22

Glazed pink linsey-woolsey quilt, backed with unglazed khaki-coloured wool. Evenly stitched hand-quilting. Parallel diagonal lines fill the negative space between flowing lines of running feather, bunches of grapes and roses.

The pink wool fabric used for the front of the quilt is believed to have been manufactured in Norwich and then exported to America.

This type of fabric is called 'linsey-woolsey', a term derived from the Middle English *lynsy wolsye* – a cotton or linen fabric woven with wool.

This Whole-Cloth quilt is typical of the earliest type of quilting in the Colonies and still retains its original glazed surface. The sheen of the pink fabric was perhaps achieved by burnishing the wool with a smooth stone. Buffing the wool after it had been coated with a mixture of egg white and water would have produced a similar effect.

The quilt is hand-quilted with very regular stitches. Snaking lines of running feather vine encircle tendrils terminating in heavy English roses in full bloom and bunches of grapes, ripe for the picking. Feather patterns border the edges of the quilt. The background space is filled with rows of diagonal lines running across the quilt.

The quilt was formerly part of a collection owned by Cora Ginsburg, a prominent New York dealer who specialized in antique fabric and costume. Acting as a consultant to several prominent American institutions, Ginsburg helped shape the textile collections at Colonial Williamsburg in Virginia – one of the inspirations for creating The American Museum in Britain.

Red Whole-Cloth Quilt

1775–1800
Eastern Seaboard, America
211 x 191 cm (83 x 75 in)
1962.22

ABOVE: Quilted silk petticoat. American, *c.*1800 (1980.65).

Red cotton and linen twill Whole-Cloth quilt, with floral motif in central medallion. Borders quilted with geometric designs. Bound and backed with the same red fabric.

Many of the earliest surviving American quilts are Whole-Cloth. They are closely related to quilted petticoats and often have the same quilting designs on them. At a time when nothing was wasted, old or worn petticoats were often taken apart and reused as the central panel for a bed quilt. Additional pieces of fabric were added around the petticoat to make it big enough to fit a bed.

The term 'Whole-Cloth' is somewhat misleading, as the tops of these quilts were rarely made from a single piece of fabric. Eighteenth-century looms did not produce wide enough cloth to make a quilt top and quilts of this type were usually pieced from many lengths of material. This top has been assembled from seven pieces of fabric,

each one a different size. The quilt was probably dyed after it had been completed, as the thread colour closely matches that of the fabric. It is possible to see the original colour of the fabric where the quilting thread has moved. The dye has also worn away along the seams joining the pieces of cloth together.

The quilted shapes on this example – a central medallion and surrounding geometric borders – are stylistically similar to many Welsh quilts. The centre of the quilt contains a circle (28 in diameter) with a rose quilted in it (see p.13). The negative area within the circle, surrounding the rose, has been filled with small, close stitches. The circle is enclosed by a rectangle (40 x 31 in), filled with diamond quilting. Three borders surround that: one with wineglass quilting (5½ in wide), the second with double-stitch diamond (3½ in wide) and the last with close parallel zigzags (8 in wide).

Glazed Worsted Quilt

1775–1800
Eastern Seaboard, America
285 x 250 cm (112 x 99 in)
1982.2

Central panel of seventy-one squares of pink, green, tan and dark indigo, set on point, within a dark indigo border (20 in wide). The border has been pieced with the bottom two corners missing to allow the quilt to hang flat on a 'post' bed. The centre and the top border have been quilted with a diagonal pattern, while the side and bottom borders have been quilted with running feather vine.

The central rectangle (79 x 59 in) is made up of squares of moreen and other eighteenth-century furnishing fabrics. These squares (7 in wide) have been set on point, with triangles sewn at the edges to give a square finish. At first the squares appear to have been pieced in a random manner. A second look, however, reveals V-shapes in the design, formed by bands of light and dark squares, with the indigo squares aligned down each side and across the top.

Brightly coloured wools were among the most coveted imported goods. These highly finished fabrics had a crisp and polished surface, as illustrated by the sheen on this quilt. The person who made this example has taken care not to

waste any of this precious fabric, with some of the squares sewn together from smaller scraps.

The quilt is backed with indigo woollen homespun cloth, and the quilt is padded with brown sheep's wool. Indigo blue is a common colour for early quilts: the colour held well and, as it was dark, showed less dirt. As with other quilts of this date, the quilting is very fine. Straight parallel lines fill each square in the centre, running at right angles to each adjoining square. The side and bottom border are decorated with an elaborate running feather vine. Flowers have been quilted in each vine arc. Close parallel lines fill the remaining areas, accentuating the feathers on the vine.

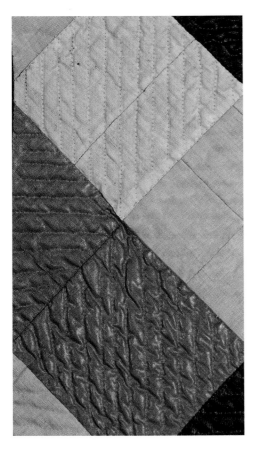

ABOVE: The pink and pale green squares have been sewn together from smaller pieces of fabric.

RIGHT: Running feather vine quilting in the left-hand border.

BELOW LEFT: The homespun backing shows colour irregularities from the dye.

BELOW RIGHT: The wool used for batting is visible through small holes in the back of the quilt.

Sawtooth Quilt

*c.*1800
New Holland, Pennsylvania
Made by Elizabeth C. Kinzer
228 x 231 cm (90 x 92 in)
1958.135

Quilt top made of white homespun with a sawtooth pattern of printed English cotton. The large pattern is repeated in miniature in the centre. The border is hand-quilted with a running feather design, which is repeated in the border of the central block. Overlapping circles (or wineglass pattern) have been quilted in the pink triangles, and the white areas are quilted with diamond filler. Label with maker's signature attached.

Only two different fabrics make up this early pieced top: one patterned and one plain. The composition still uses the medallion format, a central motif surrounded by one or more borders. The pattern is pieced from large and small triangles to create a sawtooth design. The central block has been repeated, on a larger scale, in the border that surrounds it.

The binding of this quilt is especially interesting. It has been made from short lengths of the patterned fabric, joined together with tiny white triangles, and is only seen on the front of the quilt. The outside edges of the binding (as well as the backing) have been folded in and then tacked together along the edge. This method of binding a quilt is known as 'knife-edge' in America.

The quilt top has been heavily quilted in a manner similar to Whole-Cloth quilts. Rather than accentuating the patchwork with the quilting, the contrasting fabrics act as defined areas that contain different quilting patterns. The wider white borders provide the perfect space to showcase a running feather vine. To enhance the vine, parallel diagonal lines have been stitched in the white space around it.

ABOVE: Fabric label signed by the quilter.

LEFT: Small white triangles have been inserted between each length of binding fabric.

OPPOSITE: Detail of central block quilting.

Miss Porter's Quilt

1777
Eastern Seaboard, America
Made by Miss R. Porter
244 x 231 cm (96 x 91 in)
1959.92

Pieced blocks (4½ in wide) with small eight-pointed stars alternate with plain white or patterned brown squares. Some of the plain squares and stars are decorated with embroidery. An inner border (9½ in wide) contains appliquéd swags and vases of flowers in blue and brown fabric. The appliqué border is surrounded by a pieced border (10½ in wide) of white squares, set on point, between brown triangles. This border is quilted with scallops in the triangles and diamond filler in the squares. The rest of the quilt has minimal quilting.

This is the earliest dated quilt in the collection of The American Museum in Britain. The following inscription has been embroidered in cross-stitch in the centre of the quilt: 'R— Porter, her bed quilt, made in the year 1777'. Only the 'R' of the first name is legible. Whatever Miss Porter's first name, she has used this quilt to showcase her prowess with a needle. As well as displaying her skills as a quilter, Miss Porter also demonstrates her embroidery skills on her bed quilt. Fine birds and a teapot are illustrated in stitches.

Unlike the Sawtooth Quilt (see pp.26–7), another early pieced quilt in the museum collection, Miss Porter's Quilt has a large number of blocks covering the quilt top. The quilt has an appliqué border – common in early pieced tops – but some of its other features are anything but conventional. The small areas of white visible on the baskets decorating the border have been made using reverse appliqué, whereby areas of the basket's blue patterned cloth have been cut away to reveal the plain fabric beneath.

Although the sale (but not the production) of printed cottons was prohibited in Britain for much of the eighteenth century, no such buying restrictions were imposed in America. Ironically, therefore, the rebellious colonists could purchase British printed cottons, such as those seen on this quilt – materials denied to quilt-makers in the mother country – with impunity.

ABOVE LEFT: Centre block with Miss Porter's cross-stitched inscription.

ABOVE: Small birds and a teapot have been embroidered on some of the plain squares.

LEFT: Sections of the blue appliqué vase have been cut away to reveal the white fabric beneath it.

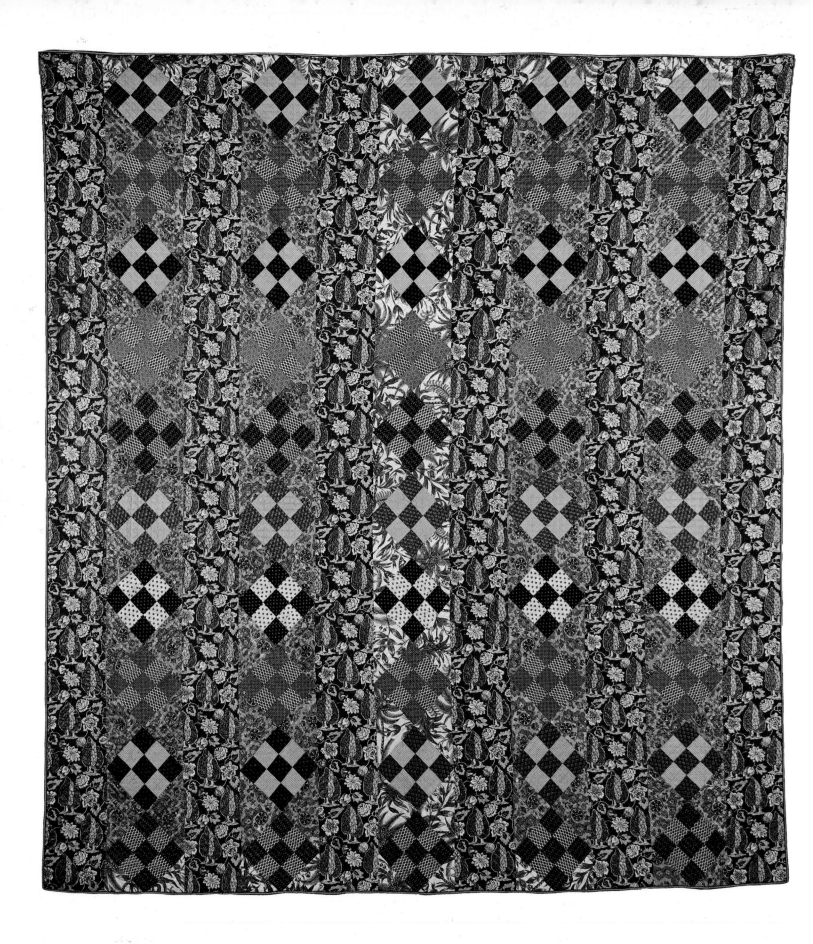

ABOVE: A selection of glazed cottons on the quilt top. Hand-woven tape has been used to bind the quilt.

Nine-Patch Strip Quilt

Eastern Seaboard, America
1817
254 x 236 cm (100 x 93 in)
1968.115

Six columns (7½ in wide) of floral chintz alternate with five bands of Nine-Patch blocks (7 in square). Each of these blocks is set on point within triangles of blue chintz. Backed with muslin and bound with hand-woven tape.

This is another early dated quilt from the collection of The American Museum in Britain. On the reverse, the quilter has cross-stitched their initials and the date: 'S.G. 1817'. It is likely that this was the date that they completed the quilt. No accompanying documentation exists and so, apart from these initials, nothing more is known of the quilt-maker.

Nine-Patch is an early patchwork block and often forms the foundation for many later and more complex designs. It has been used to great effect in this quilt, set on point within vertical stripes of chintz. The Nine-Patch blocks are positioned to form ten bands running across the quilt. These bands are accentuated by the use of the same two fabrics for all horizontally aligned blocks.

The European glazed cottons featured on this quilt illustrate the crisp details produced by copperplate printing processes in the late eighteenth century. Columns of chintz have been cut from the same fabric, with great care taken in the cutting and the placement of the adjacent rows. The triangles that complete the strips around the Nine-Patch blocks have all been cut from another fabric, with the exception of the centre band. Bright blue and white chintz that has been used for this central column stands out against the more subdued colours that surround it. Triangles at the top and bottom of each strip have also been cut from this bold fabric, again adding uniformity.

The quilting is simple but very neat. The Nine-Patch blocks have been quilted with cross-hatching. The triangles and chintz stripes are decorated with parallel zigzags running down the length of the quilt.

ABOVE: The quilter's initials and the date have been cross-stitched onto the back corner.

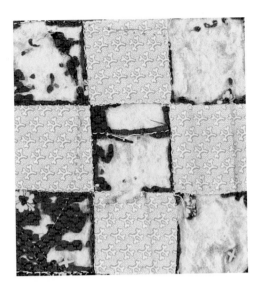

LEFT: Chintz border with knife-edge binding.

ABOVE: Some of the dyes used have caused the fabric to deteriorate, revealing the wool batting beneath.

BELOW: A selection of the many different cottons used in the quilt top.

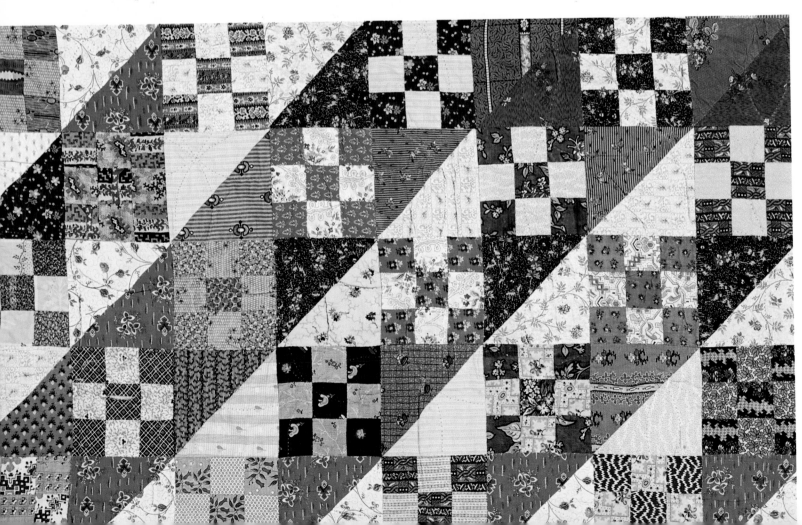

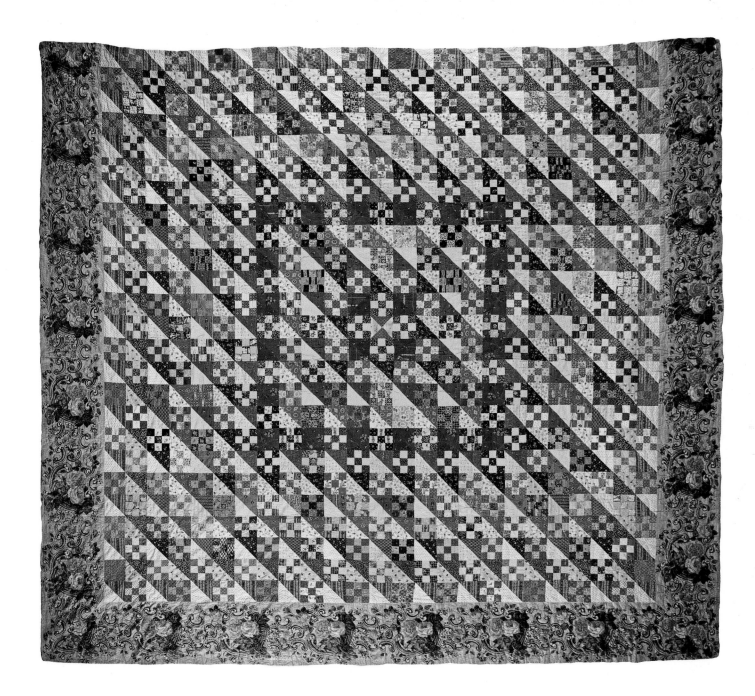

Bridal Chest Quilt

*c.*1832
Chester County, Pennsylvania
232 x 259 cm (91½ x 102 in)
1958.138

Pieced Nine-Patch blocks alternate with half-square triangles to create the effect of extended diagonal stripes. The Nine-Patch blocks (3 in square) are pieced from over a hundred printed cottons (glazed and plain). The border (10½ in wide) is English copperplate chintz. The entire quilt is quilted in overlapping wineglass pattern. Backed with brown glazed cotton and filled with wool wadding.

Made by a bride of English descent living in Chester County, Pennsylvania, this quilt is constructed from 3,556 pieces of decorated cotton, printed in the early nineteenth century. One-inch fabric squares are arranged in Nine-Patch blocks that flow in diagonal bands across the quilt. The space in between is packed with triangles, each filling half a square. Given the precision of the piecing, the fabric squares were almost certainly stitched over papers before being sewn together. Remarkably, some of the tiny squares are made from smaller scraps. Nothing has been wasted.

The scrap nature of the quilt has been somewhat tempered by the bride's use of only two different fabrics in each Nine-Patch. The chintz border has been carefully cut so that one section of repeated pattern fills the width of the border, with minimal waste. The neatly stitched quilting covers the surface in wineglass pattern. The brown thread used for the quilting blends into the various fabrics, so that the quilted decoration does not detract from the patchwork design.

Traditionally, an American girl would begin to make quilt tops for her bridal chest as soon as she became competent with a needle. The tops formed part of her dowry. Each successive example would be more complicated to piece and quilt, so the young woman could showcase her technical skill. According to custom, she would aim to produce thirteen quilt tops in preparation for her married career – the last, and most intricate, being the Bride's quilt.

Rose of Sharon Quilt

1850
New York State
Made by Lavinia Krishner
249 x 203 cm (98 x 80 in)
1959.115

Twelve appliquéd green and red Rose of Sharon blocks on white background. Wide appliquéd border of green leaves and flowers in vases. The roses have been stuffed to enhance the quilt's three-dimensional quality. The quilting design incorporates flowers and leaves with hearts.

Rose of Sharon quilts were popular during the nineteenth century and were traditionally made for newlyweds. The pattern is thought to represent romantic love and the sacrament of marriage. The name derives from the Song of Solomon:

Let him kiss me with the kisses of his mouth. For thy love is better than wine. I am the Rose of Sharon and the Lily of the Valleys …

There are many variations of the Rose of Sharon pattern. This design is the most common, with stems and buds radiating from a central rose.

The border has mitred inner corners, which is unusual for quilts of this date. (Usually borders had two longer sides and two shorter sides; mitred corners use more fabric.) The flowers have not been padded by the *trapunto* method of inserting pockets of padding through discreet slits in the backing (as used in the Colonel's Lady Quilt, see pp.66–7). Instead, additional cotton was placed underneath the red fabric roses before they were appliquéd onto the quilt top. Some of the green fabric has discoloured to a dull brown – most strikingly along the top border – which suggests that two bolts of green fabric were used.

This Bride's quilt was made by Lavinia Krishner in celebration of her marriage to John Fox in 1850. While a baby, John Fox had been taken by Native Americans and given the name 'Little Fox'. As he never learned his true identity, he adopted the name John Fox. Many years later, Lavinia's and John's initials were embroidered in cross-stitch in the border of the quilt by their daughter, along with the date of their marriage.

ABOVE: Sections of the roses have been padded for three-dimensional effect.

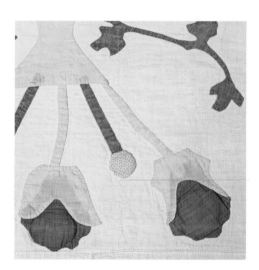

ABOVE: Some of the green fabric has discoloured to a dull brown.

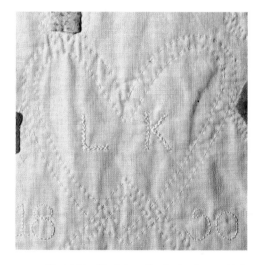

ABOVE: The initials of Lavinia and her husband were added to the quilt by their daughter.

34

Christmas Bride's Quilt

Late nineteenth century
American
188 x 188 cm (74 x 74 in)
1958.89

Quilt with appliqué design of heart-shaped holly wreaths. Each white cotton block (20 in square) contains one holly wreath and a pair of holly leaves in each corner. White cotton border (7 in wide) contains red cotton swag, with (faded) green cotton leaves appliquéd at each apex. Bound with red cotton and backed with white cotton.

The prominence of heart-shaped holly wreaths on this quilt implies that it was made for a bride on the occasion of her Christmas wedding. Including the heart motif on anything other than a bridal quilt was considered imprudent – a foolhardy action that could bring down the bad luck of spinsterhood on the unfortunate maker or recipient of the quilt.

The traditions for making Brides' quilts vary, but it was conventional for an American girl to have up to thirteen quilt tops in her hope chest. These she could begin to piece together in her youth. Custom dictated, however, that she was not allowed to back and quilt them until she became engaged. Sometimes the groom himself created an appliqué pattern for his bride to piece and quilt. Other bridal quilts were designed co-operatively by female friends and relations, who helped the bride to finish the many quilt tops in her dower chest in celebration of her marriage. Between 1775 and 1850, Brides' quilts were traditionally All-White quilts. After that date, many different patterns were used and often the only indication that these quilts were made for brides is the inclusion of hearts in the design.

The heart shapes and holly leaves have been cut from green cotton. (The green fabric has now mutated to a beige colour.) Each of the berries has been stuffed to give it a more sculptural appearance. The intricate quilting is fine and even, with the appliqué outline-quilted. Flowers have been quilted in the areas between the holly leaves, where the corners of four blocks meet. Quilted hearts echo the shape of the appliquéd wreaths. The border has been quilted with a running feather vine.

ABOVE: Appliqué swag border and red binding.

OPPOSITE: Holly heart wreath with stuffed berries.

BELOW: Elaborate quilting patterns are seen on the reverse.

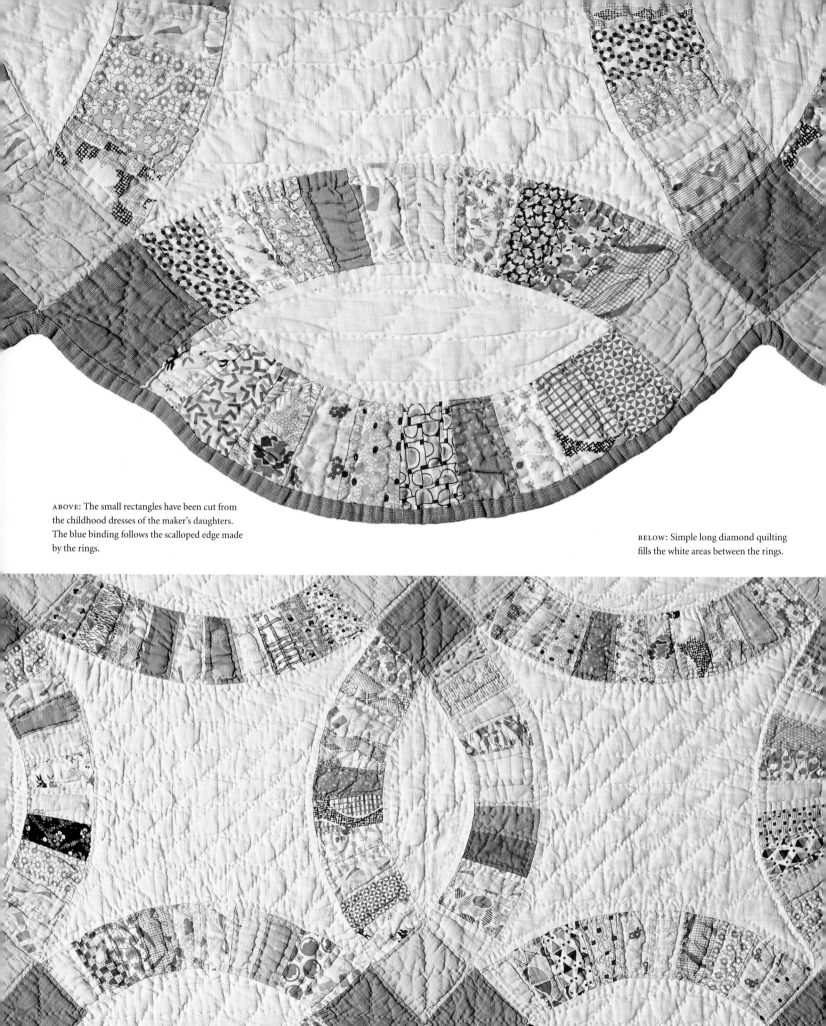

ABOVE: The small rectangles have been cut from
the childhood dresses of the maker's daughters.
The blue binding follows the scalloped edge made
by the rings.

BELOW: Simple long diamond quilting
fills the white areas between the rings.

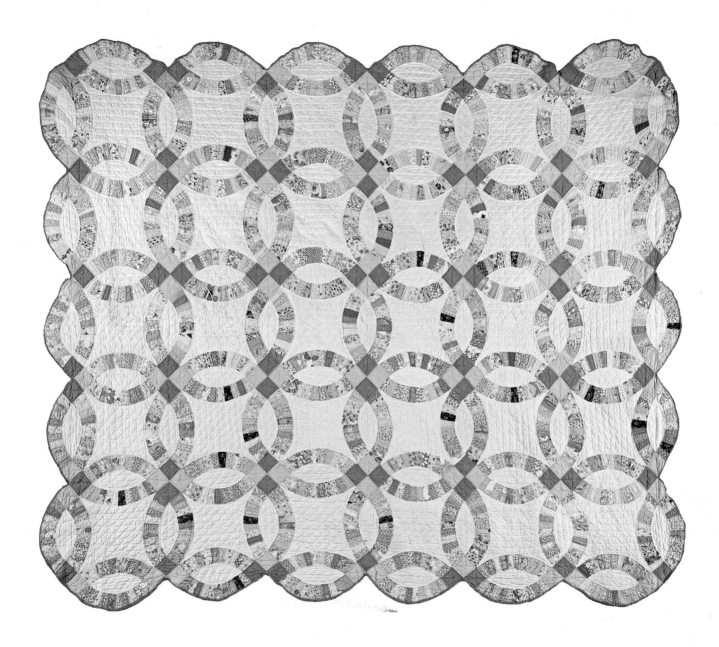

Double Wedding Ring Quilt

1930
Clarkesville, Texas
Made by Grace Munschain
196 x 224 cm (77 x 88 in)
1973.179

Interlocking circles of patterned cotton – ten pieces in each segment, with pink and blue squares at intersections. White cotton background. Backed with white cotton and bound with blue cotton. Scalloped edge follows the curve of the pieced rings.

Early Brides' quilts were made in a variety of patterns, often only distinguished as such by the inclusion of a heart motif in the piecing or quilting. In the late 1920s, a new pattern emerged that became incredibly popular for marriage quilts: Double Wedding Ring. The earliest known example of this quilt was published in 1928. During the next two decades, when the

pattern was most popular, numerous kits and designs were produced. Variations of this pattern have been found on quilts made before the twentieth century – such as Pickle Dish (another name for Lafayette's Orange Peel, see pp.64–5).

A large number of Double Wedding Ring quilts from the first half of the twentieth century exist, probably because they were treasured wedding mementoes – perhaps only used for best. These quilts are often not considered fine examples of the craft, however, and the piecing and quilting are often inferior to those made in the previous century.

The small rectangles that make up Double Wedding Ring quilts provide the perfect opportunity to use saved scraps of material. Grace Munschain from Clarkesville, Texas, pieced this example together with fabric from her daughters' childhood dresses.

LEFT: The batting of this quilt has worn so thin that fabrics on the front are visible through the backing.

Wool Appliqué Quilt

*c.*1830
New England
250 x 201 cm (99 x 79 in)
1971.17

Heavy quilt pieced with narrow strips of blue wool, which slightly overlap and thus create a ribbed effect. Flowers, birds and other motifs have been appliquéd in wool, with embroidery for the finer detail. Around the edge of the quilt is a border of geometric blue and pink woollen tongues. The backing has been replaced several times.

The centre of this quilt is an appliquéd variation of the Rose of Sharon design (see pp.34–5). This pattern was popular in the mid-nineteenth century and was often used for Brides' quilts. Closer inspection of this quilt, however, suggests that this is not the case here. The mood of the quilt is one not of joy but of sombre remembrance. In the bottom left-hand corner of the quilt is a cross that appears to be on a mound of earth (or a grave). Alongside this is an anchor, often associated with the sea but also used as a Christian symbol to represent the hope of eternal life.

The general theme of remembrance is accentuated further by other motifs present on the quilt. Pansies, for instance, stand for thoughts of lost loved ones. In Shakespeare's *Hamlet*, Ophelia, in her madness, gives them to her brother Laertes, unwittingly goading him to revenge. Referring to the story of Proserpina, the Queen of the Underworld in Graeco-Roman mythology, the pomegranate has come to symbolize immortality and resurrection. In Christian iconography, the lily-of-the-valley refers to Mary weeping below Christ on the cross, while the grapevine is a symbol of rebirth (as well as abundance).

The central pink, white and blue Rose of Sharon is surrounded by grapevines and four smaller roses in pink circles. The larger appliqué designs have blanket stitch around their edges. There is substantial staining on the quilt top, and this, combined with the fact that the backing has been replaced at least three times, suggests that this is a well-used quilt.

RIGHT: Corner of quilt with appliqué motifs symbolizing death and rebirth. Tongue edge cut from different-coloured wool.

Darts of Death
or Widow's Quilt

1860–1900
Possibly New Jersey
234 x 150 cm (92 x 59 in)
1959.4

Black and white Darts of Death blocks alternate
with plain white squares. The blocks are set on
point in a black border (2 in wide), which is in turn
surrounded by a white border (2½ in wide).
Quilted harps fill the plain squares. The black darts
are surrounded by in-the-ditch quilting.

The dynamic contrast of black silhouettes
against white suggests that this was a
Widow's quilt. The pattern derives from a similar
design known as Hosanna or The Palm. It was
popular in pre-Revolutionary America, with the
name commemorating the entry of Jesus into
Jerusalem. Widows' quilts are traditionally black
and white (or sometimes grey and white, with
a black border). They consist of simple patterns,
either a dart motif (symbolizing 'darts of death')
or a cross and star design. The quilting patterns
used tend to be weeping willow, harps or lyres.

The quilting on this example is very fine and
the quilter was certain of her skill at keeping the
stitches even. White thread has been used to quilt
the patterns and is very prominent on the black
of the darts, where she has quilted just inside
each of the sections of the dart. Found on many
early American quilts, the harp or lyre quilted in
each of the plain white blocks is an old quilting
design – one popular in northern England since
the 1600s.

Many Widows' quilts were made during the Civil
War, to be used during the period of mourning.
It is unknown how long they were made in
advance of death, if at all. Other types of
mourning quilts include examples made from
the clothes of the deceased. As well as providing
physical heat, these bedcovers would also have
given emotional comfort to the bereaved, who
could still be wrapped, metaphorically, in the
warmth of the lost loved one.

OPPOSITE: Quilted harps, a popular motif in northern
England, fill the plain squares. White quilting stitches stand
out against the black V-shapes.

Album Quilt Top

1862
Newark, New Jersey
175 x 175 cm (69 x 69 in)
1959.167

Quilt top only – not layered and quilted. Twenty-five appliquéd blocks, using either 'broderie perse' (cut-out chintz) or bold red and green silhouettes, are stitched onto plain cotton fabric. National symbols Lady Liberty and the eagle (both pictured with the Union Flag) frame the central block showcasing Psalm 23.

Album quilts are so named from their similarity to autograph albums – collections of signatures, often accompanied by poems or quotations. (Selections of suitable verses and maxims for such a purpose were conveniently printed in contemporary compilations.)

Unlike Friendship quilts, which are constructed with a repeated pattern, Album quilts are made from blocks of different designs. Moreover, the signature emblazoned on an Album quilt block would not always belong to the person who had stitched it. The blocks on this quilt top, for example, are signed by both men and women – not necessarily the makers of the blocks but possibly the friends of the person for whom the quilt was intended.

Many of the flowers and birds on this quilt top have been cut from bolts of printed chintz and appliquéd onto a plain white background. The technique of incorporating patterned chintz pieces, in a manner similar to that used in *decoupage*, was popular in eighteenth- and early nineteenth-century quilts. The technique lost popularity in America around the time of the Civil War, when more conventional appliqué designs were preferred.

The central block is by far the finest. The Bible pages are printed with Psalm 23, with the page edges delineated by tight lines of embroidered stitches. Embroidery threads have been used to shape the appliquéd flowers, with the fuchsias above the Bible enhanced further by applied pieces of pink velvet.

The theme of sleep is common to many blocks on this quilt top. Quotations from several sleep-related psalms, often used at funerals, suggest that this quilt was made to commemorate someone who had died. The date of 1862 on certain blocks and the inclusion of Lady Liberty holding the Union flag (see frontispiece) could imply that the deceased was a casualty of the Civil War – perhaps a soldier fighting for the Union or someone sympathetic to its goals.

Baltimore Album Quilt

*c.*1847
Baltimore, Maryland
314 x 314 cm (122 x 122 in)
1964.5

Appliqué Album quilt of twenty-five blocks, pieced from traditional Baltimore patterns onto plain cotton background. Each block is divided by sashing (red patterned fabric with white cotton squares, set on point along its length). An appliquéd floral vine border in red and green (14 in wide) runs continuously around the quilt, which is edged with red stepped triangles. Backed with white cotton and bound with green cotton. Cross-hatched quilting does not extend across the appliqué designs.

Of all Album quilts, those produced in Baltimore, Maryland, are the most prized – such as this flamboyant example, made for display rather than domestic use. The exceptional condition of this and other Baltimore Album quilts (many of which have never been washed and show no sign of wear) supports the idea that they were intended as extravagant gifts, with little practical purpose, which honoured the givers as much as the recipients.

The availability of new fabrics for appliqué work sparked displays of virtuosity. Vermiculate fabrics were effectively employed to emulate floral seed-heads. New *fondue* fabrics, with their gradated tonal range, gave three-dimensional shape to silhouettes of vases and bowls. Such fabrics were expensive – another proof, perhaps, that these quilts were to be considered primarily as showpieces.

The presence of two blocks featuring red keepsake books is a clear reference to the autograph or memory albums that inspired these pieces. The verse that surrounds the book motif on the left even has the title 'For the Album'. The recurrence of the same blocks in different quilts has led some historians to suggest that they may have been available in kit form or professionally designed.

The signatures on this quilt are not necessarily those of the makers. Many of the inscriptions are penned in black indelible ink (available for sale from 1840), although some initials have been embroidered in neat cross-stitch. Several names are accompanied by short verses, with themes of friendship and life in a new home.

OPPOSITE ABOVE: *Fondue* fabric has been used to give this vase a three-dimensional shape.

OPPOSITE BELOW: The album block with its inscription 'For The Album' is a clear reference to the autograph books that inspired these quilts.

OPPOSITE ABOVE: This block design showcases the delicately patterned red fabrics available at the time the quilt was made.

OPPOSITE BELOW LEFT: Every signatory has used their own unique style.

OPPOSITE BELOW RIGHT: Block with dedication to Mrs Howe.

Friendship Quilt

1847
Crescent City, Maryland
Made by the ladies of St George's Church
251 x 251 cm (99 x 99 in)
1958.88

A selection of red and white printed calicos is used to make over a hundred eight-pointed star blocks. Many of the white background squares and circular star centres are signed and dated. Two rows of red triangles, facing inwards, form the border. The lines of these triangles are set apart to form a white zigzag between them. Very simple hand-quilting. Backed and bound with plain white cotton.

Signature quilts that use a repeated block design to create a pattern over the quilt top are called Friendship quilts, to distinguish them from the elaborately appliquéd Album quilts. The fashion for Signature quilts originated in Pennsylvania and Maryland in the early 1840s. Interest in making this type of quilt fluctuated throughout the remainder of the nineteenth century, although the style regained some lost popularity in the later decades.

The craze for Signature quilts coincided with the fad for red and white quilts. Consequently many examples use red and white patterns – the latter providing a perfect setting for inscriptions. This quilt showcases the delicately patterned red fabrics available at the time. Care has been

taken cutting pieces for the stars to ensure that directional patterns all radiate out from the centre. The simple outline quilting enhances the stars and the white square blocks contain a quilted teardrop in each corner.

One of the blocks contains the inscription: 'Friendship offering to Mrs Howe by the ladies of St George's Church 1847.' Why this quilt was made for Mrs Howe is uncertain, but such quilts were often presented as mementoes to people moving away from a community that valued them. The blocks on this example have been signed by different people, rather than being inscribed by one individual selected for the task by virtue of their elegant handwriting. Short verses or delicate stamps accompany the signatures.

"I have yet have been young I never but now righteous am old. Forsaken."

John Sutton, Sr.

1849

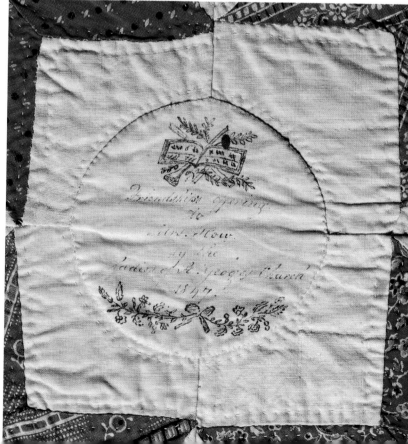

Robbing Peter to Pay Paul Quilt

*c.*1889
Oriskany Falls, New York
**Pieced by Connie Chard and quilted by the ladies
of the Congregational Church**
215 x 206 cm (85 x 81 in)
1963.18

*Red and white Friendship quilt – each of the white
pieces has a signature in it. Two dates are inscribed
on the quilt: 1886 and 1889. Hand-quilting
outlines the red shapes and forms a grid through
the centre of the white sections. Backed and bound
with white cotton.*

This complex-looking design uses only two
different blocks placed in different directions
to create the pattern. Once the basic block has
been mastered, the pattern is simple to create.
A fan-shape has been cut from the white block
and added to the red, while the section cut from
the red block is added to the white block. The skill
lies in turning the block through ninety degrees
to ensure the continuance of the pattern.

This block design has several names, including
Rocky Road to California and Drunkard's Path.
The red 'pathways' formed by the arrangement
of the blocks clearly inspire these road-related
names. The blocks make a bold pattern and the
simple quilting does not detract from this eye-
catching design.

There are nearly four hundred inscriptions on
the quilt. The individuals named did not sign it
themselves; instead, the signatures were added by
Victor J. Nye, who was assisted by his wife. It was
not unusual to have one person responsible for
the inscriptions on a Friendship quilt, particularly
if they had good handwriting. The quilt top was
pieced by one person, Connie Chard, in 1889.
Her name is signed on one of the blocks. As no
single person is identified as the quilter, it is likely
that several members of the church helped with
the quilting.

ABOVE: Block showing the names of the person who pieced
the quilt and the two people who inscribed the names.

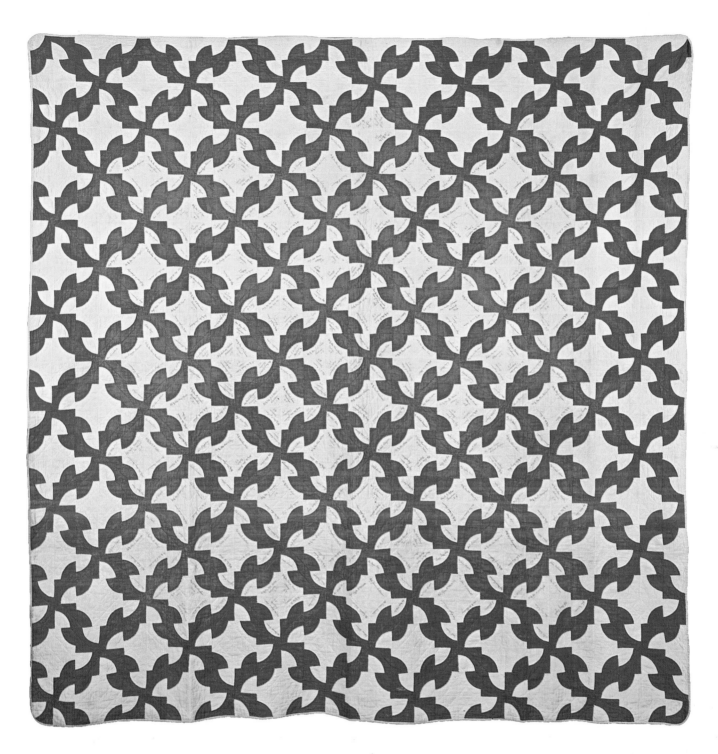

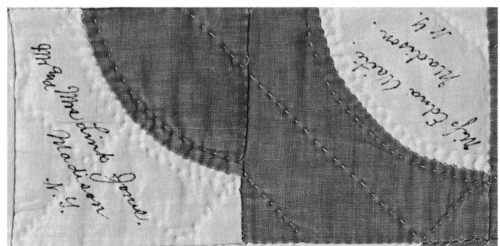

RIGHT: Two blocks make up this design: a white square with a red corner and a red square with a white corner.

Mosaic Friendship Quilt

1848
Shepherdstown, West Virginia
234 x 264 cm (92 x 104 in)
2008.1

Quilt top pieced from hexagons in Grandmother's Flower Garden pattern. Each of the ninety 'flowers' has a signature, sometimes accompanied by a handwritten inscription or stamped design in its centre hexagon. Cream cotton has been used for the 'paths' between the flowers. A chintz border

(4½ in wide) runs around the edge of the quilt. Backing and binding of plain cream cotton. Feather quilting along the hexagon paths and straight parallel lines are quilted diagonally across each of the flowers.

Made in Shepherdstown, Virginia, and dated 1848, this Signature quilt features a colourful collection of commercial chintz fabrics that had only recently become affordable through new industrial processes. This type of quilt was

often made as a joint effort in the mid-nineteenth century to commemorate a special event, to raise funds or to honour the contribution made by an individual to a community.

The dates inscribed on the blocks range from 25 January to 9 September 1848. Many of the signatures are accompanied by verses with a Christian theme, some taken directly from the Bible. On 6 January 1848, the Feast of the Epiphany, a committee of the Old Reformed

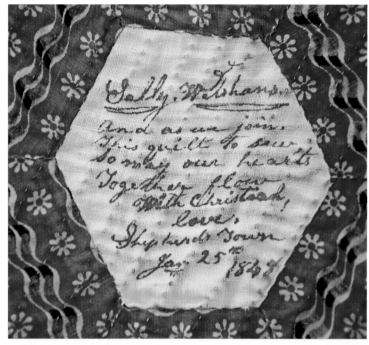

Church of Shepherdstown agreed to introduce catechism to church school classes. One of the signatories on the quilt, Joseph Welshans, was the secretary and treasurer of the governing board of the church. His wife and children also signed blocks.

Several blocks have the inscription 'remember me', suggesting that this quilt may have been made as a memento for a respected member of the community (as this type of quilt often was).

Owing to its biblical references, it is thought that this quilt could have been made for a pastor or as a raffle prize to raise funds for a local church. Although the name of the person that made this quilt is unknown, one inscription indicates that it may have been pieced by more than one person:

And as we join / This quilt to sew,
So may our hearts / Together flow
With Christian / Love.

TOP LEFT: Hexagon signed by Joseph Welshans, secretary and treasurer of the governing board of the Old Reformed Church.

TOP RIGHT: Sally Welshans's inscription, 'And as we join this quilt …'

BOTTOM LEFT: Inscriptions of 'remember me' suggest this may have been made for someone leaving the community.

BOTTOM RIGHT: Some signatories have used small stamps to decorate their blocks.

54

Mosaic Diamonds Quilt

1861
Charlie's Hope Plantation, Southampton
County, Virginia
Made by Anne Eliza Urquhart (née Blunt)
267 x 254 cm (105 x 100 in)
1972.272

Quilt top pieced from hexagons arranged in a repeated diamond pattern. The multicoloured diamonds are separated by a unifying border of green hexagons. Hand-quilted with straight lines that dissect each point of every hexagon. Bound with dark green patterned fabric and backed with pieces of natural linen (joined by hand).

Hexagons are one of the oldest patchwork patterns: dated examples survive from the eighteenth century. The popularity of hexagons increased in the following century. In 1835, *Godey's Lady's Book* published a Honeycomb quilt design. Early nineteenth-century quilts used small hexagons, sometimes no bigger than one inch across, as an opportunity to parade the new printed fabrics that were becoming available.

Hexagon quilt tops are pieced using the paper technique. Uniformly sized hexagons are cut from paper. The fabric is then cut a quarter of an inch wider than the paper hexagons and secured, turning the edges to the back of the paper. Once these fabric hexagons (filled with paper templates) have been made, they are arranged in the desired pattern and whip-stitched together. When the pattern is complete, the initial basting stitches are cut and the papers removed.

The assembly of this quilt is very intricate and patterns change according to viewpoint. The hexagons have been arranged in diamond shapes, with two rows of different fabric surrounding the central hexagon of each diamond. The diamonds are separated by rows of hexagons made from plain green fabric. The points at which the green rows intersect are marked with single red hexagons. Reading these red hexagons as central medallions, the diamonds radiating outwards from these junctures form six-pointed stars. From another perspective, the diamonds also form a variation of the Tumbling Blocks pattern.

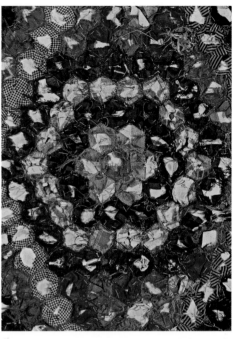

ABOVE: Unfinished hexagon quilt top. American, nineteenth century (1973.184). The papers used to form the hexagons are still present in this unfinished quilt top.

RIGHT: Patriotic flag fabric has been used in this arrangement.

ABOVE AND RIGHT: The hexagon diamonds are arranged in six-pointed stars (above) or Tumbling Blocks (right), depending on the perspective of the viewer.

ABOVE: The chintz border has been meticulously cut to fit the printed pattern. Woven tape binds the top to the backing.

LEFT: Each hexagon is one inch wide. Care has been taken, when cutting the fabric for the hexagons, to ensure that the pattern is in the centre of each one.

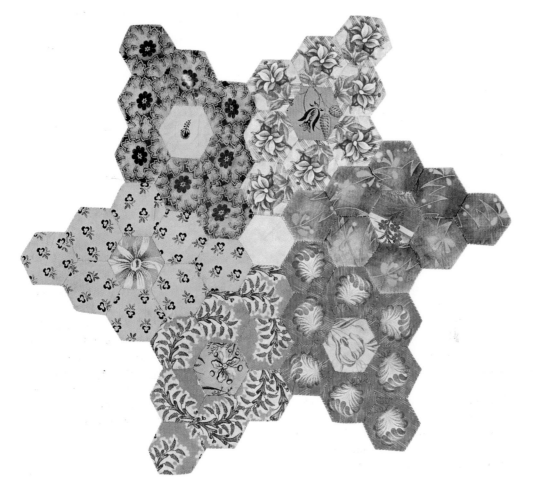

Chintz Summer Bedspread

*c.*1830
Drayton Hall Plantation, South Carolina
330 x 330 cm (130 x 130 in)
2005.22

Lightweight for summer use, this bedspread is decorated with pieced hexagons (1 in wide) arranged in flower and star patterns on a white cotton background. The top is divided into four squares and eight triangles (two in each corner) by chintz sashing (4 in wide). A different chintz border (7 in wide) has been applied around the whole coverlet, which is backed with white cotton and bound with woven tape.

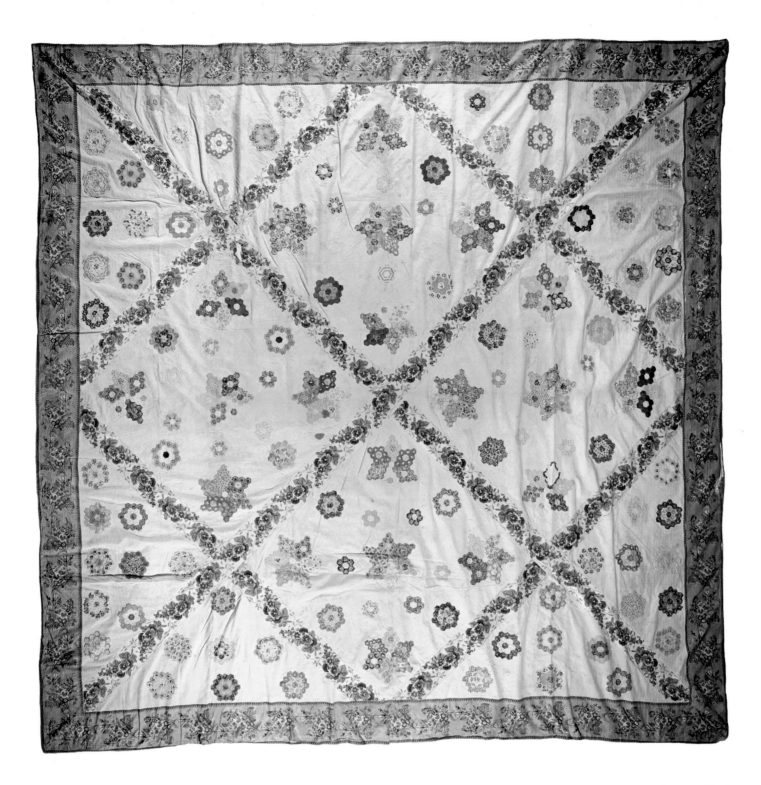

This coverlet has no middle layer and is not quilted. It has none the less been backed with white cotton. Woven tape binds the front and reverse sections together. This type of quilt is known as a summer bedspread. Usually such coverlets did not have a backing: their edges were simply finished with binding. The lightness of such a bedspread would have been preferable, in the muggy climate of South Carolina, to a thick one with batting.

The top has been pieced from tiny hexagons, only an inch across. Each hexagon has been precisely placed and stitched to ensure that the fabric pattern is shown to best advantage: flower buds, acorns and abstract designs are positioned in the centre of each hexagon. The same attention to detail is evident in the sashing, which has been cut to fit the repeated floral pattern in a vine formation along the length. The border has also been meticulously arranged to ensure the floral pattern fits the width.

The consideration that has been applied to the selection and piecing of the fabrics is the hallmark of a skilled needlewoman. A paper label attached to the quilt states that it was made by a slave seamstress living on the Drayton Hall estate –

a rice plantation, with many slaves working in the fields. Other slaves worked as coopers, blacksmiths, carpenters and domestic servants. It was not unusual for skilled slaves to work solely as seamstresses. Generally the names of quilt-makers are seldom recorded. The identities of several slave seamstresses, however, are documented. One of these women, Elizabeth Keckley, bought her freedom with money made from her sewing skills and later became the dressmaker for President Lincoln's wife.

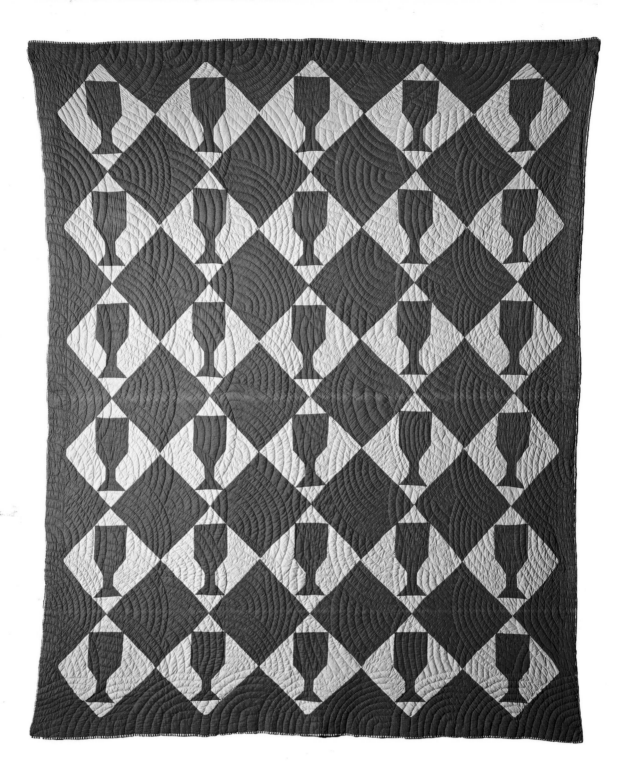

The Chalice Quilt

*c.*1860
Mimosa Hall Plantation, Marshall, Texas
221 x 191 cm (87 x 75 in)
1983.172

Thirty white blocks with red pieced chalice-shaped motif (each 8½ x 9 in), set on point and sewn by hand, alternate with solid red squares. Three pieces of machine-stitched red and white striped cotton form the backing, which has been folded around the edges to bind the quilt. Semicircles, hand-quilted in white thread, decorate the entire surface.

This quilt was made by slaves on the Mimosa Hall Plantation in Marshall, Texas, for the use of the Anglican bishop of New Orleans. Each year, the bishop would tour the region's cotton plantations to perform baptisms and marriages. After his departure, quilts made for his visits were given over for slave use.

Every slave freed represented a victory against slavery. In the early nineteenth century, a loose network of individuals who zealously shared this sentiment organized what became known as

the Underground Railroad, which ran from the south to the northern free states and Canada, through Philadelphia and New York (its two key 'stations'). Escaped slaves were progressively led at night to stations, or safe areas, by 'conductors'. Many of these conductors were Quaker abolitionists. Some were freed slaves, who risked much more than their white counterparts by returning to the south.

Historians have argued for and against the popular notion that quilts encrypted with coded

ABOVE: The striped backing had been folded to the front and stitched in place to form the binding.

RIGHT: The fan shapes quilted over the whole piece differ in size; they are significantly smaller down the middle of the quilt as can be clearly seen on the reverse.

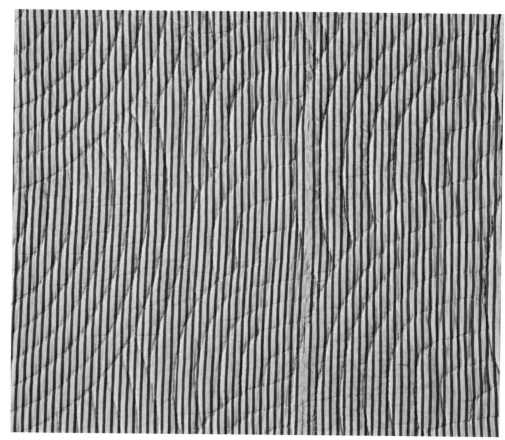

patterns (such as the Bear's Paw, Wagon Wheel, Crossed Monkey Wrenches and Log Cabin) were strategically hung along the routes of the Underground Railroad. Although the decoration of this quilt does not conceal codes for the railroad's conductors, it none the less contains a hidden message. The repeated motif of the chalice represents not only the bishop but also, more importantly, the freedom of a better world to come, after a life of blood and suffering.

ABOVE: The name 'Elizabeth Karen' has been stamped onto one of the blocks.

LEFT: This corner of the quilt shows where the piece has been cut up and sewn back together. A section of the border is missing, and many of the stars have been abruptly sliced off.

BELOW: The politically themed backing fabric shows Harrison below a log cabin.

Tippecanoe and Tyler Too Quilt

*c.*1840
American
203 x 188 cm (80 x 74 in)
1958.4

White cotton blocks (7½ in wide), each containing an eight-pointed star of coloured fabrics. The blocks are set on point within an English chintz border (6 in wide). The quilting is an all-over pattern of fans. The backing fabric is American printed cotton with a political theme. The name 'Elizabeth Karen' is stamped onto one of the blocks.

This quilt derives its name from the politically themed fabric used for its backing. It features the slogan 'Harrison and Reform' underneath a likeness of the ninth President of the United States, the Whig William Harrison, who governed

for only thirty-one days. Other images on the fabric include a log cabin with a cider barrel alongside – symbols adopted by Harrison and his running mate, John Tyler, after their Democrat opponents claimed that Harrison was only fit to 'sit in his log cabin drinking hard cider'.

'Tippecanoe and Tyler Too' was the title of a campaign song used by the Whigs during the 1840 presidential election. Harrison was known as 'Tippecanoe' following his victory in 1811 at the Battle of Tippecanoe, part of Tecumseh's War. After his victory over the Native Americans, Harrison was acclaimed a national hero – despite the fact that his troops greatly outnumbered their opponents and suffered more casualties. Harrison's presidential campaign focused on his military achievements and characterized him as

a humble frontiersman. (He actually came from an aristocratic Virginian family.)

This must have been a much loved quilt, as it has been re-stitched after worn areas were removed. Two of the original edges are still in place and can be identified by the stars that are along the edge – each triangle contains exactly half a star. The other two edges have been cut and show only fragments of stars. By matching the fabric of the star motifs, it is possible to work out the original length of one side (96 in). The reverse sections that have been altered are more decipherable, as the printed pattern is upside down or placed sideways. It is clear that these repairs were made after the quilt was finished as the quilting is now interrupted by seams.

Whig's Defeat Quilt

1844–55
Tennessee
226 x 274 cm (89 x 108 in)
1999.154

*Six full Whig's Defeat blocks and three half blocks
of yellow, red and green fabrics pieced and
appliquéd onto white background. Floral appliqué
border of roses similar to those on Whig Rose quilts.
All hand-sewn and hand-quilted. Green binding.
Backing pieced from three sections of cream cotton.*

The blocks used in this quilt top are also known
as Sunflower, Broken Circle and Indian Summer.
After the defeat of the Whig party in the 1844
election – in which the Democrat candidate,
James K. Polk, triumphed over the Whig
candidate, Henry Clay – the block featured in
quilts that were called Whig's Defeat.

Whig's Defeat is a celebration of Polk's victory.
It is often pieced from red, white and blue fabric
to emphasize the patriotic nature of the design.
It has been argued that the appliquéd plumes at
the points of each block represent the tail feathers
of a rooster – the bird being, at that time, the
symbol of the Democratic Party. The roses in the
border are similar in style to those that make
up the Whig Rose blocks. This pattern was
appropriated by Democrat supporters and, in
1845, renamed Democratic Rose.

Great skill was needed on the part of the person
who assembled the quilt top. The yellow and red
bands require a high degree of accuracy when
piecing to ensure that the points of the diamonds
are not lost. Similarly, the appliqué plumes must
be sewn carefully to retain their sharp shape.
Unlike the intricate piecing, the quilting itself is
uncomplicated: outline quilting is used around
the coloured pieces, long diamond filler covers
the white background and straight parallel lines
(in groups of four) define the border.

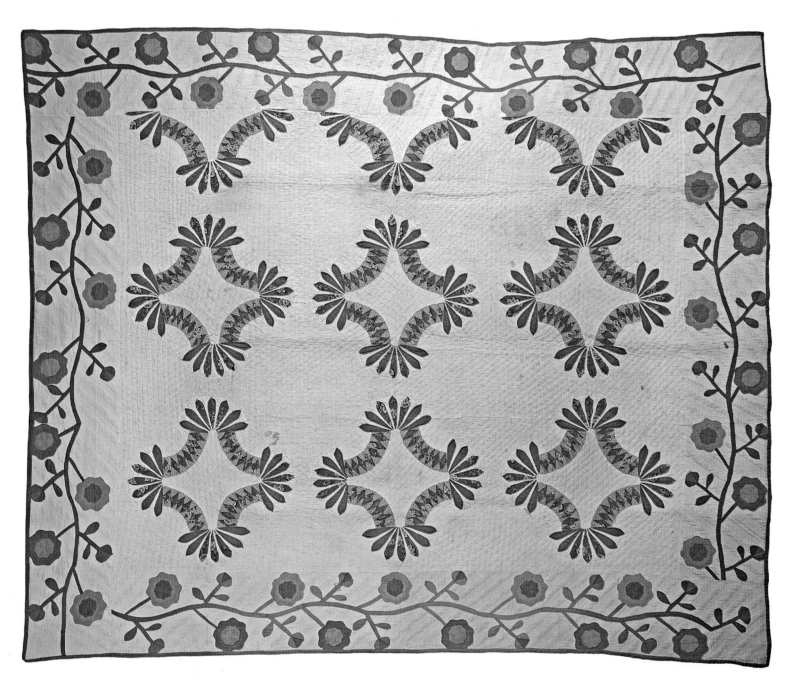

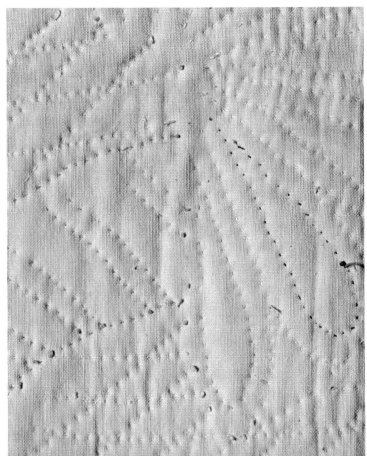

ABOVE: Great skill is needed in constructing this block to retain the points of the diamonds and the shape of the appliqué plumes.

LEFT: Different colour threads have been used for the quilting and are clearly visible on the back.

RIGHT: The appliqué rose border shows the uneven nature of the green dye in the fabric used.

64

Lafayette Orange Peel Quilt

1830–75
American
239 x 201 cm (94 x 79 in)
1996.2

Indigo blue cotton fabric with white polka dots has been used in conjunction with white cotton to make the blocks (7½ in square), which are pieced together on point. The border (5 in wide) is not uniform: two sides are indigo blue with white ovals, while the other two sides are the inverse of this (white with blue ovals). Contour quilting echoes the design.

The Marquis de Lafayette was a popular hero of the American Revolution. A French general, he served in the Continental Army under George Washington. His success in the Revolution made him popular among Americans and many new towns and cities were named after him.

This pattern derives its name from an anecdote about Lafayette. Soon after the American Revolution, a celebratory banquet was held at which oranges were served. Lafayette was among the guests and it is said that he quartered his orange before peeling. One of the female guests was so enraptured by the evening that she took his orange peel segments home and designed a quilt block with them. It is unlikely that this story is anything more than a popular myth, as each version of the tale is slightly different. Other names for the pattern include Pincushion, Bay Leaf, Tea Leaf and Lover's Knot.

The blocks for this quilt are constructed in a manner similar to that of Robbing Peter to Pay Paul (see pp.50–1). Four segments are cut from the blue square and sewn onto the white square, while the segments cut from the white square are sewn onto the blue one. These squares are then alternated to produce an overall pattern of circles. This pattern of circles has led some quilt historians to suggest that it is an early version of Double Wedding Ring.

RIGHT: A seemingly simple block design creates a complex-looking pattern.

The Colonel's Lady Quilt

1821
American
Made by Mary Waldron Thompson (née Nexen)
269 x 226 cm (106 x 89 in)
1963.10

White Whole-Cloth quilt with stuffed design.
Central medallion contains Lady Liberty under the
outstretched wings of the emblematic eagle, with
seventeen stars above. Close quilted diamonds fill
the space between the central image and the floral
designs. Three sides of the quilt are fringed, as well
as either end of the top edge.

A hallmark of the wealthy, who had the resources to keep them clean, early nineteenth-century All-White quilts provided the means for accomplished needlewomen to display their dexterity. This quilt uses the techniques of stuffing (*trapunto*) and cording. *Trapunto* was popular in America at the end of the eighteenth century and during the first half of the nineteenth century. Small slits have been cut in the back of this quilt – where stuffing has been inserted – and then discreetly re-stitched.

All-White quilts traditionally have a central medallion that is surrounded by one or more borders of floral or geometric design (see p.69). The subjects pictured in the medallion varied. This quilt features Liberty, adorned with her cap and wielding the Union flag, encircled by symbols of martial might (drum, cannon and cannon-balls). Above her is a spread eagle holding an olive branch in its beak, surrounded by seventeen stars. Although the number of stars suggests a date for this quilt of 1803 (when there were seventeen states in the Union), this is not the case.

The fact that Mary Waldron Thompson was the wife of a soldier may explain the military and patriotic nature of its decoration. Her husband was Colonel Alexander Thompson and she accompanied him to frontier forts in what was then known as 'Indian Territory'. They were the hosts of General Lafayette at Fort Niagara, when he visited during his celebrated tour of America (August 1824 to September 1825). After her husband's death, Mrs Thompson lobbied Congress to provide pensions for the widows of army officers.

TOP: Mary Waldron Thompson added her initials (M.W.T.) and the date, 1821, to the top of the quilt using cording.

CENTRE: Cording knots are visible on the back of the quilt.

BELOW: Small slits have been cut into the back of the quilt to enable extra padding to be added to some sections. They have been stitched up after stuffing.

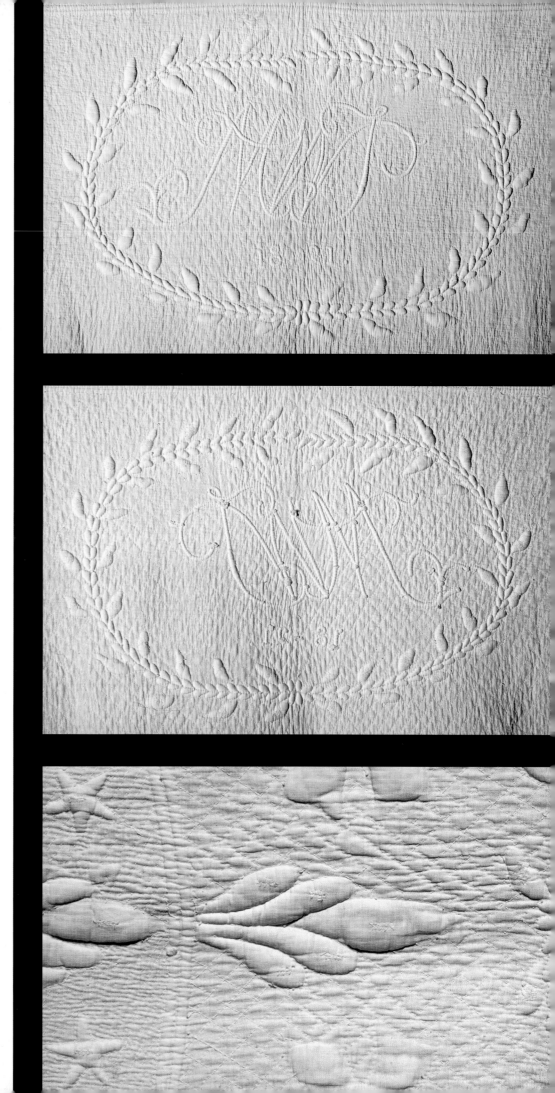

OPPOSITE BELOW LEFT: Black fabric (with a delicate pattern of pink roses and vines) has been used for the quilt backing.

OPPOSITE ABOVE: Eagle from Album Quilt Top (also featuring Lady Liberty, see frontispiece and pp.44–5).

OPPOSITE BELOW: The central medallion of The Colonel's Lady Quilt contains Lady Liberty with military motifs underneath a spread eagle. (see pp.66–7).

Union Quilt

*c.*1885
Northern states
200 x 193 cm (79 x 76 in)
1958.109

Four plump eagles with olive branches in their beaks are appliquéd to the corners of a bright orange background, surrounding a central star. The grey-brown fabric was originally green. The eagles have been quilted with parallel lines echoing the diagonal placement of the birds. The red border has been quilted with a cable design, and the rest of the quilt is covered in long diamond filler. The fabric on the back is black with small pink flowers.

Union quilts were extremely popular during the 1860s, especially in the northern states. Most Union quilts were made in Pennsylvania. As in this example, they often featured the eagle – a symbol of the United States since the late eighteenth century. Here, however, the composition is unusual. The emblematic bird is not the expected centrepiece. Instead, four eagles decorate this piece, each aligned to a different corner. A stylized star occupies the centre of the quilt.

Despite the eagle being a favourite pictorial subject for quilts, there is no geometric design for it, as there is for other birds (such as Goose Tracks or Flight of Swallows). As a consequence, all eagle designs are appliquéd or quilted. Depending on the skill of the individual quilt-maker, therefore, representations of the emblem of the Great Seal could look more like commonplace farmyard fowls (as in this example).

Appearances can none the less be deceiving. In a letter to his daughter in 1784, Benjamin Franklin argued that the lowly turkey would be a much more fitting symbol of America than the seemingly noble eagle. Franklin declared the eagle a 'rank Coward' and thought the turkey 'though a little vain and silly, a Bird of Courage [which] would not hesitate to attack a Grenadier of the British Guards who should presume to invade his Farm Yard with a red coat on'.

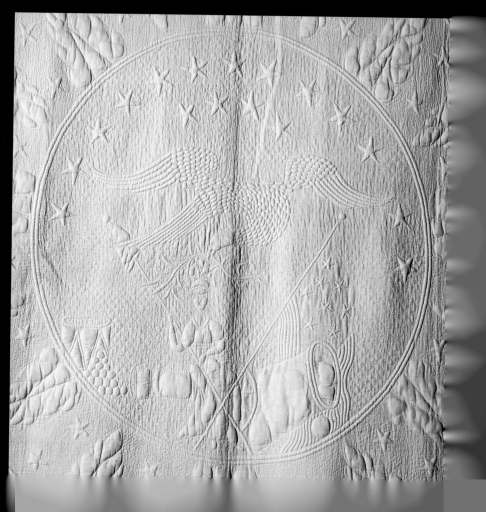

Eagle Appliqué Quilt

*c.*1963
American
240 x 200 cm (96 x 80 in)
1998.156

Gold cotton eagle appliquéd onto white background. The eagle holds flowering branches, with thirteen stars above its head. Intricate floral designs have been appliquéd around the eagle and a swag border has been appliquéd to the edge of the quilt. Hand-quilted in gold thread.

This quilt (based on a chintz version made in 1795) has been made by hand from a kit sold by the quilt pattern makers Paragon, which included fabric recommendations and instructions for making the quilt. The white cotton quilt top onto which the design has been appliquéd is made of five pieces of fabric hand-pieced together. The backing is of the same gold colour as the design on the front. The quilt does not have any binding. The edges of the front and back have been folded in and stitched together. Gold thread has been used for the quilting – an indication of the confidence of the quilter, whose neat stitches thus stand out distinctly against the white background.

The eagle is the most frequently used of all birds in pictorial quilt patterns and is a common design in patriotic quilts. In 1782, Congress adopted the eagle as the emblem of the Great Seal of the United States. This led to a fad for the eagle as a design motif. Eagles appeared on all manner of decorative arts, including furniture, ceramics, glass and textiles. Patriotic use of the eagle went out of fashion during the 1840s but was revived during the Civil War.

Quilts that feature the eagle as the central design motif are known as Liberty quilts. Most were made between the Revolution and the late 1830s. The stylized eagle is appliquéd in the centre of the quilt and surrounded by a wreath of stars.

The number of stars almost certainly represents the number of states in the Union at the time the quilt was first made, a reference to the original Thirteen Colonies.

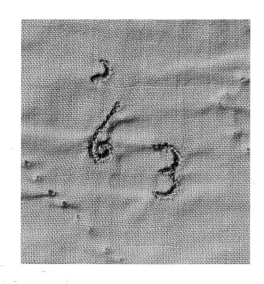

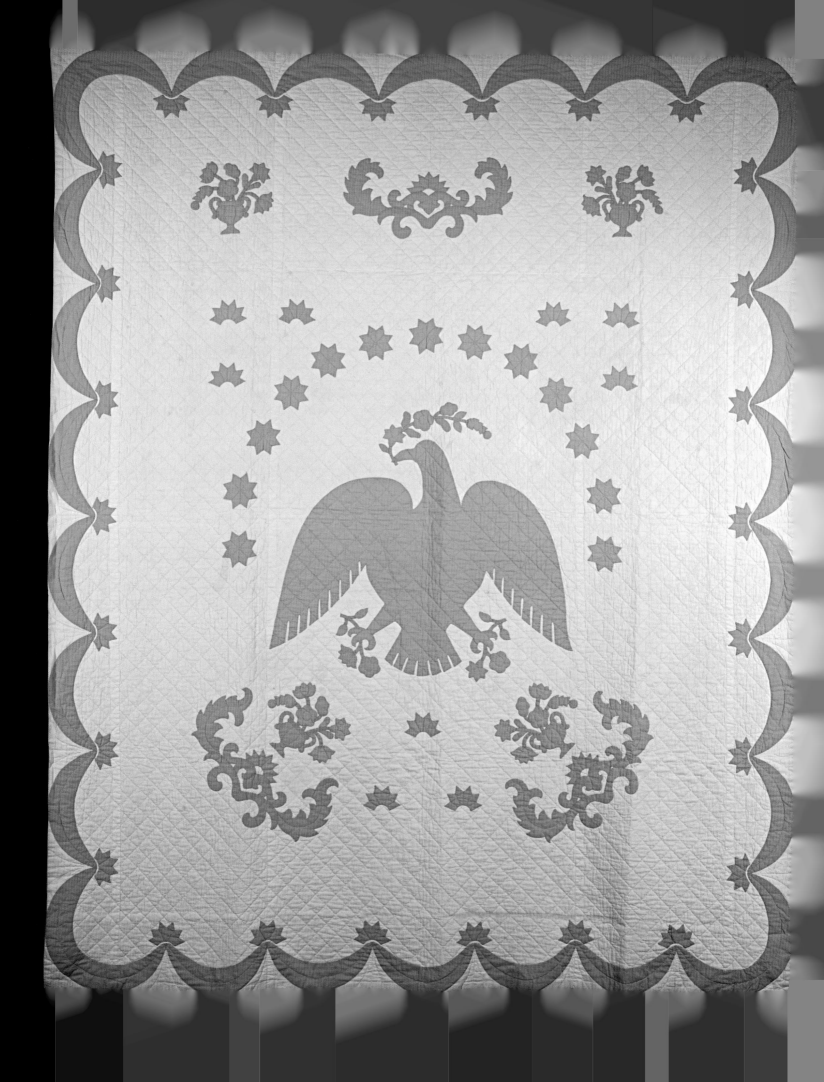

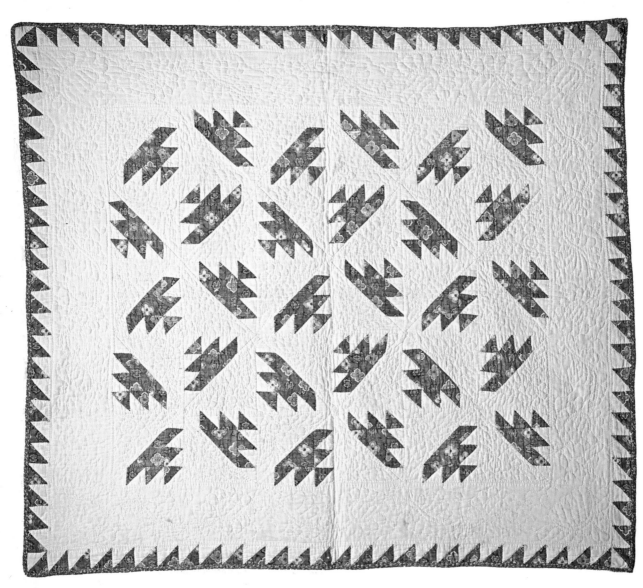

OPPOSITE: The sailboats
have been assembled
using half a Swallow
block and a plain white
half-square triangle.

BELOW: The binding
fabric along the top edge
is a different pattern,
indicating that it may be
a scrap of new fabric that
replaces a worn-out edge.

Sailboats Crib Quilt

1840–1900
America
89 x 101 cm (35 x 40 in)
1976.54

*Crib size quilt – thirty Sailboat blocks of red
patterned cotton and white cotton. The blocks are
surrounded by a white cotton border (4 in wide),
which has been finely quilted with flowers and
leaves. A sawtooth border made of the same fabrics
used in the blocks (1½ in wide) completes the quilt,
which is bound with red fabric and backed with
white cotton. The quilt is hand-pieced and
hand-quilted.*

This small quilt was made for a crib and has
been well used. The fabric has puckered
around the quilting stitches, probably owing to the
number of times it has been washed. Repairs have
been carried out on the quilt: the binding along
the top edge has been replaced with new fabric of
the same red colour but in a different pattern.

Each block is composed of large and small
triangles cut from plain white and red patterned
cotton. The pattern is made using half of the
Swallow block with a plain white triangle. From
the 1880s, the women's magazine *Hearth and
Home* advertised new designs for quilt patterns
and this block design is illustrated under the title
'Lost Ship'. The fabrics, however, seem to date
from around 1840. Either the quilter made this
crib quilt at the end of the nineteenth century,
sewing fabric that had been squirrelled away, or
the pattern was known before the 1880s but
produced commercially only after this time.

Each block has been quilted in-the-ditch, with
additional straight lines following the diagonals
of the red triangles. Stylized flowers have been
quilted in the white triangles and white border.
The border also contains a running feather vine.
No doubt the quilting on this piece was densely
stitched to ensure that the quilt would withstand
heavy use.

Pine Trees Quilt

1875–1900
Pennsylvania
203 x 196 cm (80 x 77 in)
1962.15

Machine-pieced blocks (11½ in square) with pine tree design are set on point and alternate with plain white blocks. Four alternating borders (each 1 in wide) of red and white cotton surround the quilt. Backed with white cotton and bound in red cotton. Hand-quilted with scallop filler on pine tree blocks, feather wreath design on plain blocks and diamonds in borders.

Tree emblems have been a popular image in American quilts for as long as they have been made. Wealthy colonists used *palampores*, bed-spreads imported from India. These were decorated with designs inspired by the natural world: animals, birds and plants. A popular design was the Tree of Life. This motif, in turn, influenced eighteenth-century *broderie perse* quilts. These often had a large central image (an arrangement of flowers or a tree) cut from printed chintz and appliquéd onto a plain background. This trend declined in popularity before the Civil War and was replaced by pieced designs.

The huge forests of the New World may also have inspired tree designs in quilts. The pine tree is a symbol of the forests of New England, which provided tall masts for the king's ships. The importance of the pines to early settlers is demonstrated by the 'pine tree shilling', one of the first coins struck in the Colonies.

The Pine Tree pattern is one of the earliest pieced patterns to have survived unaltered through the centuries. The precise piecing of the blocks has ensured that all the triangle points are visible. The blocks have been set on point, placing the trees upright on the quilt rather than on a diagonal. Feather wreaths with diamond filling have been quilted in the plain white blocks between the trees.

OPPOSITE: The blocks have been pieced on-point so that the trees stand upright. Delicate feather wreaths adorn the plain blocks that alternate with the pieced ones.

ABOVE: Borders with diamond quilting and binding.

LEFT: A variation of the Tree of Life motif, the Cherry Tree design was especially popular at the beginning of the twentieth century.

Cherry Trees Quilt

1925–30
Oregon
Made by Naomi Beckwith
206 x 200 cm (81 x 79 in)
1997.110

In each quarter, a cherry tree is appliquéd onto a white background. The trees grow inwards from the top and bottom of the quilt, forming partial reflections of each other from above and to the side. Flanking each tree trunk is a pair of birds (one orange, one red). Appliquéd yellow flowers point inwards along the axis, while red and orange buds are positioned on diagonals between corners. An appliquéd grapevine borders the quilt, which is backed with plain cotton.

This bright quilt top is constructed from four large blocks, each with a cherry tree, birds and flowers appliquéd onto it. As with many complex appliqué designs, the quilting has been kept simple. Straight parallel lines run across each block of the quilt. In some of the large blank areas, birds and grapes have been quilted to echo the appliqué designs. There is no binding on the quilt: the edges of the front and back have been folded in and sewn together.

The Cherry Tree design – a reinvention of the Tree of Life motif – was popular at the beginning of the twentieth century. Commercial patterns were available for quilts and embroideries. In 1922, *Ladies Home Journal* sold a transfer pattern for this quilt design. The quilt pattern makers Bucilla also produced a kit (albeit a simplified version). The resemblance of this quilt to others in The Art Institute of Chicago and at the Denver Art Museum implies that this example was made using such a kit or commercially produced transfer pattern.

Another variation of the Cherry Tree Quilt was exhibited at the 1933 Chicago World's Exposition. It was made by Maggie Smith of Louisiana, who named her entry 'Our George's Cherry Tree'. Inspired by the apocryphal story of the first President's boyhood misdemeanour, Maggie included an unorthodox motif alongside her flowering trees – a hatchet.

ABOVE: Flying Geese strip, surrounded by chintz border and woven binding.

RIGHT: Smaller stars break up the plain white expanses in the corners of the quilt.

BELOW: A selection of printed cottons create radiating bands of colour.

Star of Bethlehem Quilt

*c.*1835
Bethlehem, Pennsylvania
254 x 264 cm (100 x 104 in)
1958.86

Eight-pointed star in centre of quilt, made from rows of diamonds pieced in alternating bands of colours and appliquéd onto a white background. Smaller eight-pointed stars are in the four corners. A Flying Geese border of yellow triangles on a red background runs along each side and across the bottom. A patterned chintz border, with corner blocks made of red and yellow fabric, frames the entire quilt.

Star of Bethlehem is among the oldest of patchwork designs. The pattern has several names, which relate to the geographical provenance of individual quilts. Star of Bethlehem, for instance, is commonly used in north-eastern American states; an earlier name (and one sometimes used in England) is Mathematical Star. In Texas, the design is known as Lone Star – the nickname for that state.

This stunning quilt has been pieced from diamonds (cut from patterned cotton and sewn over papers) to form a star. The skill in making such a quilt lies in the care taken in sewing these diamonds together. Small errors in stitching are exaggerated as the quilter moves towards the points of the star. These can result in the quilt having an uneven finish. This particular example, which is flat and square, has been precisely pieced.

In order to accommodate the points of the central star, the quilt is of considerable size, with (potentially) large areas of white in the corners. To add more colours and reduce expanses of plain fabric, four stars have been pieced from slightly smaller triangles and appliquéd onto the corners. All of the stars have been outline-quilted in neat stitches. The off-white background in each corner has been quilted with scallop filler. Running hammock quilting fills the remaining white background.

Sunburst Quilt

1875–1900
St Cloud, Minnesota
Made by Elizabeth Mitchell (née Cannon)
183 x 165 cm (72 x 65 in)
1966.261

Sunburst design pieced from diamonds in radiating bands of colour. The sunburst is on a yellow sateen background. Surplus diamonds have been used to make a small floating border around the sunburst. The whole quilt is confidently quilted by hand. Diagonal parallel lines fill the sunburst design; intricate floral designs and a running feather pattern fill the yellow areas. Backed with red cotton. The yellow sateen has been folded to the back and stitched into place to form the binding.

This variation of Star of Bethlehem is called Sunburst and is pieced in the same way, with each fabric diamond basted over paper before being sewn together into the desired pattern. The diamond arrangement terminates before extending out into the (more customary) eight-pointed star. The overall composition is as explosive as a supernova.

As this design does not have large points, the finished piece is smaller than is usual for star quilts. The diamonds have been appliquéd onto a yellow sateen background. Its shiny surface complements the quilting designs in red thread. The pencilled designs that guided the quilting are still visible in many areas.

Thick wadding and the use of contrasting thread enhance the quilting design. The central sunburst has been quilted in yellow thread, with close parallel lines radiating out from the centre. Stylized flowers and leaves in red thread fill each yellow area around the points. In two of the corners, roses have been quilted in red thread; the other two corners have tulips. The stunning border of running feather vine is quilted in red thread – a bold contrast to the yellow fabric.

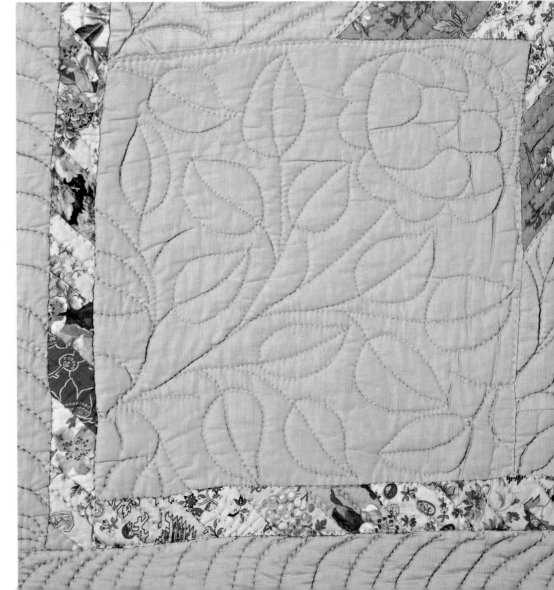

ABOVE: Red cotton used as backing shows the fine quilting.

BELOW: The quilting in red thread stands out against the yellow sateen. Pencilled lines marking the design are still visible underneath the stitches.

New York Beauty Quilt

1900–25
Ohio
198 x 175 cm (78 x 68 in)
1981.11

Pieced quilt top for single bed. The piecing is in red and plain yellow fabric; the background is white with a small black polka dot. Two parallel lines of yellow and white triangles, divided by a white line of equal size, form a border at the top and bottom of the quilt. Backed with plain white cotton. Hand-quilting echoes the pattern, while diamond quilting (¾ in apart) fills the background fabric.

This complex pattern has been pieced by an accomplished quilter. It is a difficult pattern to sew accurately, consisting of many curves and small triangles with sharp points. The colour choice is subtle. Usually New York Beauty quilts are made from bold, solid hues that enhance the graphic quality of the design.

The pattern is also called Crown of Thorns. The quilt top features four large 'crowns' of red and yellow fabric. The blocks are all joined by diagonal bands made by rows of yellow and white triangles that appear to lie over the crowns. Stars made of yellow and red diamonds mark the points at which these bands cross one another (at the centre of the crowns).

At the end of the nineteenth century and the beginning of the twentieth, companies were producing cheaper material. Although this meant that fabric was more widely available, quality suffered. Cloth from this period commonly has a lower thread count. New chemical dyes were produced, increasing colour range. Not all of these dyes, however, were stable. The chemicals used for dark colours often reacted with the fabric and caused structural deterioration. The quilt illustrates this type of damage. All pieces of the red fabric are uniformly covered in small holes. It is likely that this is a result of a mutating dye used to produce a small pattern, now obliterated, on the original cloth.

LEFT: Careful piecing ensures no points are missing from this complex block design. Small holes are visible over the surface of the red fabric, probably owing to chemical mutation in an overlaid dye.

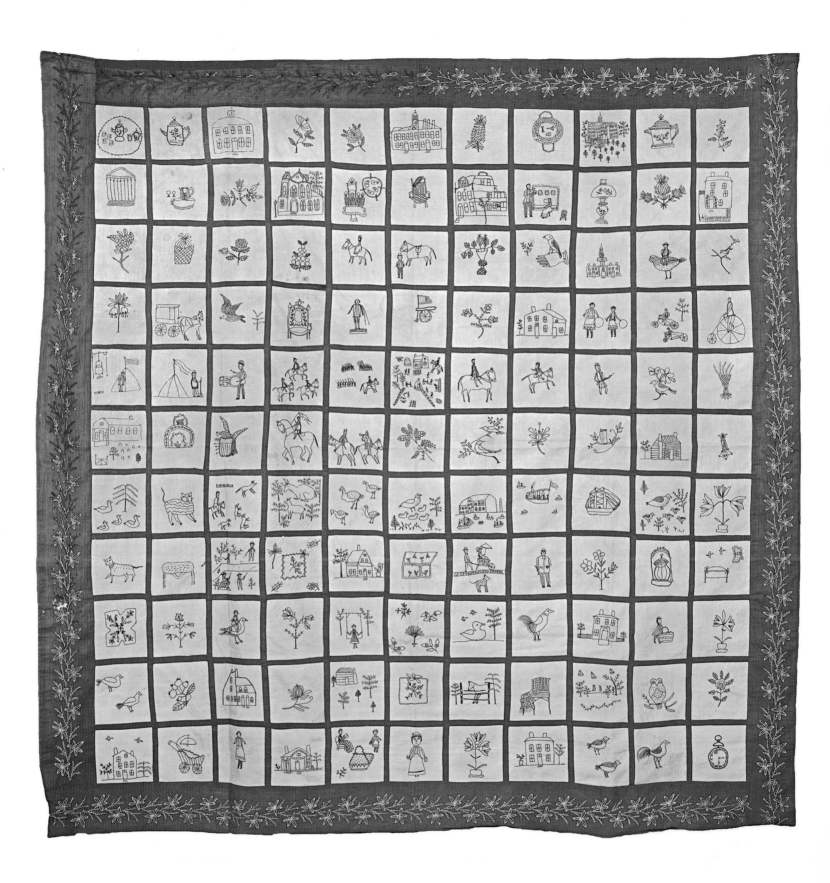

Redwork Quilt Top

After 1881
Pennsylvania
236 x 236 cm (93 x 93 in)
1960.66

Quilt top only. Over a hundred blocks of natural cotton, embroidered in red with scenes of everyday life and objects. Each block (6½ in wide) is joined with red sashing. This plain red fabric is used for the border (6 in wide), which has a floral design embroidered in white thread.

Redwork became popular during the second half of the nineteenth century. The development of a colourfast red dye (known as 'Turkey red') and the low cost of cotton led to a boom in the number of red and white quilts being made. Inexpensive materials meant that those with less money could engage in this hobby. Even people not accomplished at drawing could undertake redwork, because 'penny squares' – with pictures already printed on them – were sold in stores for a penny a piece.

It is doubtful that the blocks in this quilt were made from penny squares. The pictures have a rough (but jocular) quality about them, which contrasts with the neatness of the stitching. The even nature of the small stitches suggests that the blocks and border were all embroidered by the same hand. The design in the border is more assured and was perhaps copied from a template.

This fascinating object juxtaposes domestic scenes with those of a military and patriotic nature (including a portrait of George Washington). One block shows what appears to be a man riding a penny-farthing backwards. This is, however, probably a depiction of the 'American Star' two-wheeler. Produced by the Smith Machine Company in 1881, this bicycle had a large wheel at the back of the vehicle and a small wheel at the front.

CLOCKWISE FROM TOP LEFT: Images depicted include military camps, George Washington and a church; domestic scenes feature a girl on a swing and a tea tray; other quirky images include a man sitting on a giant bird (possibly a carousel ride), the 'American Star' two-wheeler bicycle and a woman being pushed in a wheelbarrow.

Crazy Patchwork *Portière*

1887–90
Manitoba, Canada
Made by Saedia Smith Johnson
183 x 119 cm (72 x 47 in)
1972.288

One of a pair of curtains made from Crazy patchwork in silk, velvet, ribbon and brocade. Silk embroidery stitches cover the seams and add embellishment. Some of the animals featured have been painted onto plain silk. The brown backing fabric has pulled around to the front on some edges. There is no binding; the front and back have been folded in and sewn together.

The 1876 Centennial Exposition, held in Philadelphia, was the first World's Fair in America. It was organized not only to celebrate the centenary of the signing of the Declaration of Independence but also to showcase culture and design from around the world. Illustrating the decorative arts of Japan, the Japanese Pavilion was one of the most popular attractions at the 1876 Centennial Exposition. Some quilt historians believe that Crazy quilts are the result of Japanese influence. Many of the ceramics displayed in the Japanese pavilion had crackle patterns in the over-glazing, which gave these pieces a 'shattered' finish. It is believed that the desire to recreate this broken asymmetrical design was what prompted the production of Crazy quilts.

This *portière* is one of a pair of door curtains made by Saedia Smith Johnson. Having few friends in Manitoba to occupy her time, Saedia embarked on this intensive quilting project. Despite being well used and made from fragile materials, these curtains are in remarkably good condition. In the top left corner is embroidered 'January, 24th .87.'; the lower left corner contains the inscription 'Finis August 1890'.

The quilt is full of examples of Saedia's skill as a needlewoman and accomplished artist. She has used a variety of threads to create unusual embroidery effects, even stitching pictures with thick chenille wool and thin ribbon. Several pictures have been painted onto silk, including an elephant and a finely detailed parrot. Even hooks and eyes from clothing have been used to create a delicate spider's web or dandelion head.

ABOVE: A painted parrot and elephant adorn silk scraps and are surrounded by elaborate embroidery.

BELOW: Spider web or dandelion head made from hooks and eyes.

BELOW: The silk in the top left-hand corner has shredded, revealing the foundation fabric beneath it.

OPPOSITE: Fan blocks alternate with Crazy patches. Fine embroidery embellishes the sumptuous fabrics. The rich blocks are accentuated by the striking black and white ice-cream cone border.

Crazy Fan Quilt

1875–1900
Fort Leavenworth, Kansas
Made by Mary Elizabeth Plowman
168 x 168 cm (66 x 66 in)
1980.68

Pieced from silk and velvet scraps, twenty-five Crazy patchwork and Fan blocks (11 in square) make up this sofa throw. As well as having heavy embroidery along the seams, several pieces of fabric have been embellished with embroidery and painted flowers. Backed with purple silk. Stunning ice-cream cone border of black velvet and white silk (5 in wide).

This quilt was made by Mary Elizabeth Plowman, whose father was Judge Thomas Plowman of Baltimore, Maryland. After the Civil War, he was posted to Fort Leavenworth, Kansas. During his trips back to Baltimore, he bought silks and other dress fabrics for his wife and daughters. This throw has been pieced from the scraps left over from these dressmaking activities, with the remnants thus representing particular members of the family.

The size of this quilt suggests that it was never intended as a bedcover but was made to accessorize a piece of furniture. Many so-called Crazy quilts were sewn for use in parlours as slumber robes, lap throws, piano or table covers. In keeping with the Victorian love of knick-knacks and decorative clutter, these quilts were a riot of rich fabrics, ribbons, embroidery and other embellishments. They provided a canvas for women to show off their skills as needlewomen. Indeed, the American women's periodical *Godey's Lady's Book* encouraged quilters to use as great a variety of stitches as possible.

Rather than simply displaying the traditional feather stitch, an assortment of ornamental stitches adorns the seams of this example. Various pictures have been embroidered over the quilt top, including a splendid peacock and exquisitely detailed flowers. The dynamic contrast in the border of regimented black and white conical shapes (with seams overlaid with purple feather stitching) creates the perfect frame for this quilt top by enhancing its richness even further.

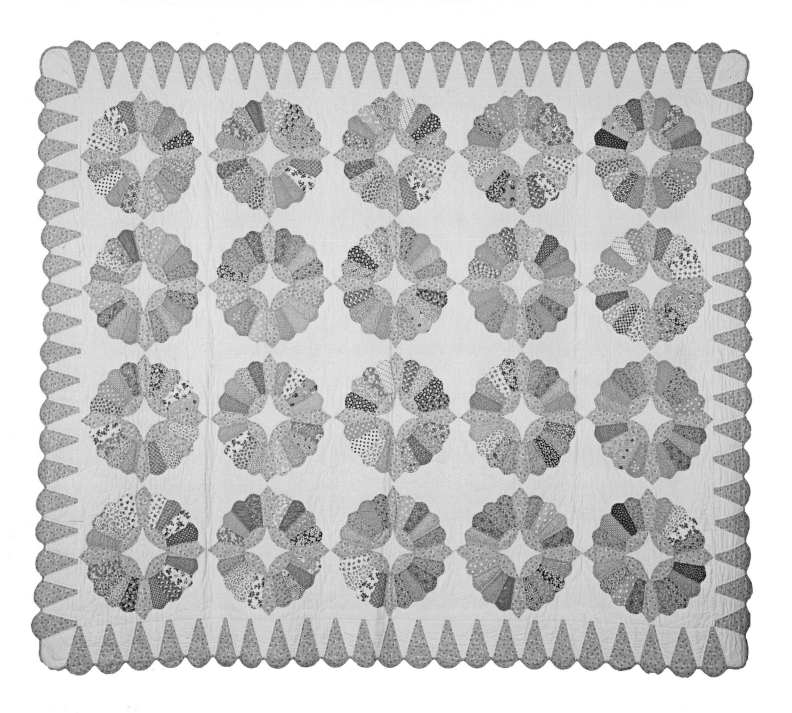

Dresden Plate Quilt

1930s
Berkeley, California
**Pieced by Marie Miller Farwell and quilted by
the ladies of Northbrae Community Church**
201 x 239 cm (79 x 94 in)
1985.167

*Twenty Dresden 'plates' pieced from pastel
patterned cottons. Ice-cream cone border in
alternating white and yellow patterned fabric.
Backed with white cotton and bound with the
yellow fabric used for the border.*

Pastel fabrics are typical of quilts produced
during the first part of the twentieth century.
Old patterns were given a modern twist by
incorporating these fabrics, brighter than the
dark materials traditionally used. The Dresden
Plate pattern is a reworking of the Fan block,
which became popular at the end of the
nineteenth century: four Fan blocks have been
placed together at the corners to form a circle.
Each plate segment has been cut from pastel dress
fabric, sewn over papers and then stitched to its
neighbours. Once completed, the individual plates
were appliquéd onto a plain white cotton block.

This example has been given an extra twist by the
way yellow material is used. Every plate is
dissected into quarters by this fabric, producing,
in effect, the appearance of a yellow cross in each
block. This material has been used to make the
ice-cream cone border – an embellishment often
featured on Dresden Plate and Fan quilts.

One person did all the piecing for this quilt.
The quilting, however, was undertaken by several
people: the ladies of the Northbrae Community
Church. Each section of fabric has been outline-
quilted. The centre of each plate has two circles
quilted into it. This circular design is repeated in
the white, stylized star shapes (reminiscent of
Mariner's Compass patterns, see pp.92–3)
between the plates.

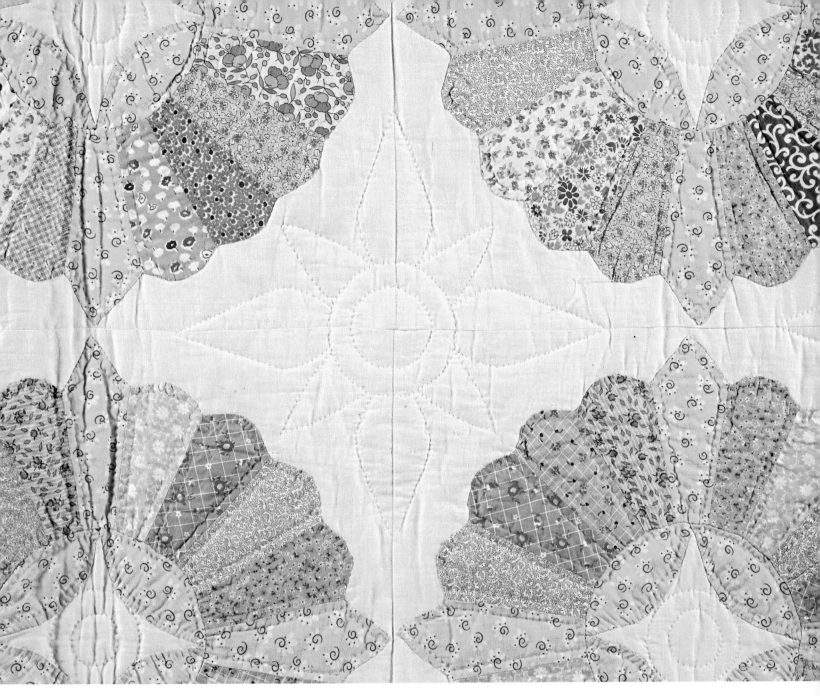

ABOVE: A quilting pattern, reminiscent of Mariner's Compass (see pp.92–3), has been stitched in the white spaces between the plates.

RIGHT: Fan blocks form the basis of Dresden Plate: four 'fans' are placed together to make a circle. This Fan Quilt (1980.70) was made by Katy Clark Elmore of Chula, Missouri, in 1937.

OPPOSITE: Bold colours, popular in Pennsylvania, lend themselves to this design.

Mariner's Compass Quilt

1825–50
Pennsylvania
264 x 264 cm (103 x 103 in)
1972.158

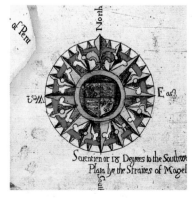

ABOVE: Compass Rose detail, 1589, from the map collection of The American Museum in Britain (1988.125).

Five full and eight partial Mariner's Compass blocks in blue, green, red and yellow fabrics, set between red and white sawtooth border. Appliqué oak leaf design at the point where sawtooth strips intersect. Inner border of red and white sawtooth. Outer border of green appliqué swag. The background fabric is cream with a small blue floral print.

Mariner's Compass is one of the earliest block designs and was possibly inspired by compass roses drawn on early sea charts or on engravings of maps included in the published accounts of voyages. The first Mariner's Compass quilts featured the block as a large central design. In later quilts, the block was small and repeated to cover the quilt top. With its strong graphic nature and opportunities for bold colour combinations, it is one of the most popular Pennsylvania-Deutsch ('Dutch') patterns.

It is uncertain when this quilt was assembled. The fabrics date from the 1820s and 1830s. The machine-pieced backing suggests that the quilt was completed after 1850. The fabric was possibly hoarded for later use, or the quilt top, first made in the 1830s, may either have been set aside at that time or its backing renewed at a later date. What is conclusive, however, is that an accomplished quilter has pieced this top, ensuring that all of the compass points are sharp and visible.

This example is almost identical to one in the collection of the Pennsylvania Quilt and Textile Museum; only the border differs slightly. Some of the red fabric has deteriorated and been repaired in places. Cotton batting is visible through the areas that have not been repaired. The quilt has been bound by turning the backing fabric to the front and hand-stitching it in place.

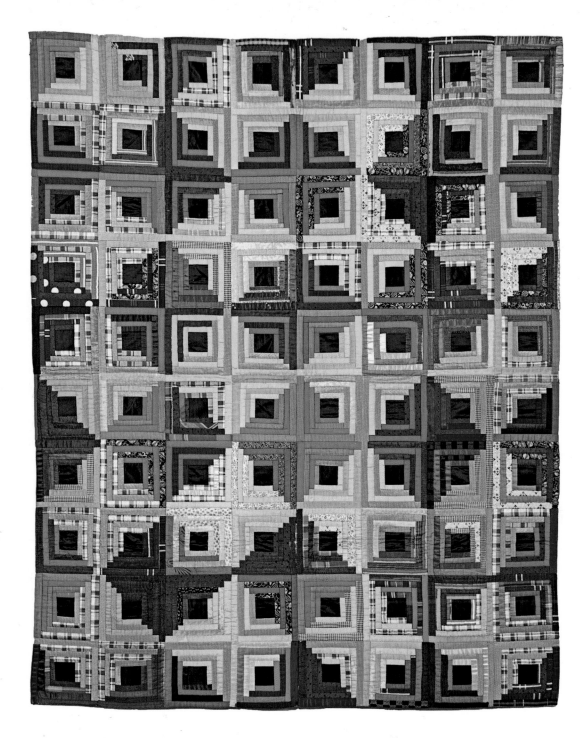

Log Cabin Quilt – Light and Dark Variation

1875–1900
Illinois
Made by Mary E. Sexton Mann
165 x 133 cm (65 x 52 in)
1981.10

Eighty Log Cabin blocks – ten down by eight across – arranged in Light and Dark pattern. Each strip is cut from silk ties and measures half an inch in width. Backed with grey silk. The edges have been folded in and stitched together.

Log Cabin is the most recognizable of all quilt blocks and the one most strongly associated with America. Given its popularity, it is surprising that the origins of the Log Cabin pattern are unknown. Most Log Cabin quilts date from between 1850 and 1889. So many thousands of these quilts were made in the mid-nineteenth century that, by the 1870s, Log Cabin had its own category in quilt contests at state fairs.

The blocks are foundation-pieced from strips of fabric cut from silk ties. A central square (usually red or yellow, but sometimes black) is sewn to a foundation fabric (or scrap paper) with the Log Cabin design drawn onto it. Each strip is then stitched to the paper and folded back over the seam, so that the pattern extends outwards until the block is complete. This method enables the quilter to achieve a very precise finish. Light fabrics are used on one half of the block, dark fabrics on the other. Depending on how the blocks are arranged, different patterns can be achieved.

The blocks of this quilt have been composed in a variation known as Light and Dark. The overall effect is one of light and dark diamonds alternating across the quilt top. Each strip is very thin, only half an inch wide. The number of seams and the foundation fabric add stability and bulk to the quilt, making quilting and batting unnecessary.

Log Cabin Quilt – Barn Raising Variation

1863–86
Londonderry and Mount Holly, Vermont
Made by Ellen Bryant Smith and Sarah Bryant
203 x 193 cm (80 x 76 in)
1971.16

Narrow cotton strips (almost ½ in wide) have been used to construct basic Log Cabin blocks, which have been pieced together to form the Barn Raising pattern. The backing is also pieced, with sixty squares (7 in wide) pieced from half-square triangles, divided by floral printed cotton sashing. Bound with red cotton.

This spectacular quilt top was pieced by Ellen Bryant in 1863, in preparation for her marriage in Londonderry, Vermont. Over three hundred Log Cabin blocks (each 4½ in square) have been arranged in a variation known as Barn Raising, with the light and dark bands radiating out from the centre of the quilt. (The Barn Raising pattern is also known as Sunshine and Shadow.)

The backing is as visually arresting as the front. It was pieced by Ellen's sister Sarah Bryant, of Mount Holly, in about 1886. The different completion dates for front and back suggest that

the final version of the quilt was assembled over two decades after Ellen's wedding. The back is made from hundreds of minute scraps of different cottons. These fragments have been cut into tiny half-square triangles and then sewn together to form larger squares. The centre block is pieced together from even smaller triangles. A strip of green patterned fabric runs along the top and bottom edge of the back.

There is no quilting, nor has the quilt been tied. As there is nothing anchoring the top to the back, other than the binding, this has caused some minor structural distortion.

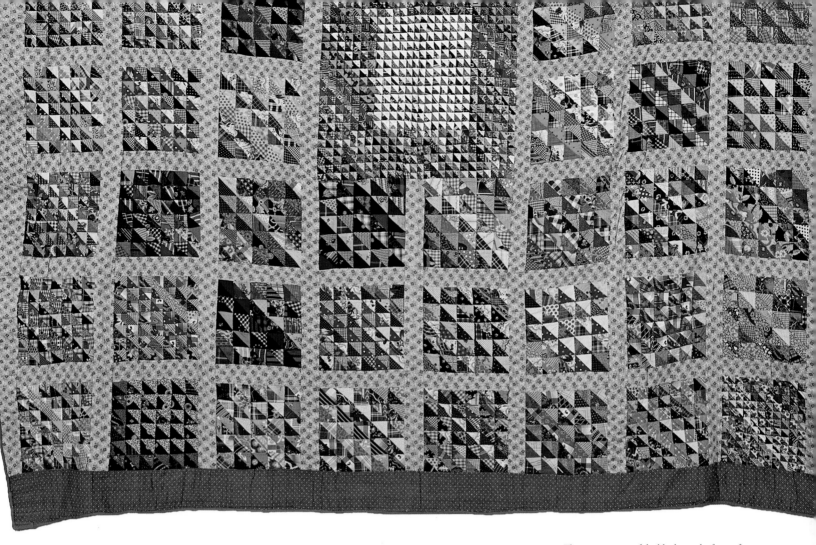

ABOVE: The back of the quilt has been pieced from hundreds of tiny pieces of fabric.

BELOW: The arrangement of the blocks on the front of the quilt creates radiating bands of light and dark.

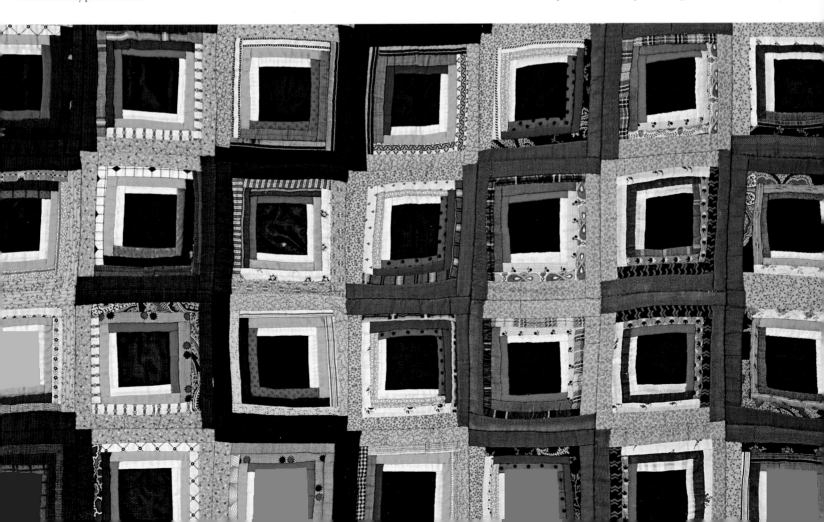

Log Cabin Quilt – Pineapple Variation

1870s
Marshall, Michigan
Made by Ethelind Amelia Washburn (née Ward)
127 x 76 cm (50 x 30 in)
1963.17

Small silk quilt constructed with the variation of Log Cabin known as Pineapple (so-called because of its spiky appearance). The edge has been trimmed with silk 'tongues'. The piece has been backed with gold silk, pre-quilted by machine for commercial sale.

This variation of Log Cabin is called Pineapple or Maltese Cross. The strips are sewn around the central square in a different pattern from the traditional Log Cabin block, with each strip ending in a diagonal edge. By using the same black silk for all the dark sections of the block, the cross design is accentuated in this example.

This small coverlet was probably made as a decorative piece. It has an amusing border – a random sequence of 'tongue' shapes cut from the many silks used in the central decoration. As is common with Log Cabin examples, this one is not quilted. The method of piecing these coverlets made them too thick to be quilted by hand, although they were sometimes tied. The backing is a commercially quilted silk of 'antique gold'. Although ostensibly produced for lining outerwear, such as gentlemen's cloaks and jackets, this luxuriant pre-quilted fabric was readily adopted for backing such coverlets.

In this quilt, the middle of each block is made from black silk. Traditionally, Log Cabin blocks have red or yellow centres. These represent the hearth of the home (red) or a candle in the window (yellow). The log cabin block is then built up around this central square, with the lighter-coloured strips standing for the sunny side of the house and the darker strips, the shady side.

LEFT: Commercially quilted silk (produced for lining outerwear) was often used to back silk quilts.

OPPOSITE: Tongues cut from silk ties form the border. Another name for this design is Maltese Cross, so-called because of the cross motifs formed by the block placement.

Cigar Silk Ribbon Quilt Top

*c.*1880
American
104 x 104 cm (41 x 41 in)
1964.338

Cigar silk ribbons have been foundation-pieced to a backing fabric, in the same manner as Log Cabin quilts. The seams have been decorated with feather embroidery stitches – an embellishment popular during the Victorian period and particularly present in Crazy quilts of the time. The ribbons have been arranged in such a manner as to suggest a Square-in-a-Square patchwork design.

During the late 1800s, cigar companies tied bundles of cigars with silk ribbons, which had the name of the company or cigar manufacturer stamped on them. Finer cigars sometimes had the name woven into the silk. As cigar-smoking was a common activity, most households had a plentiful supply of these ribbons.

The bright gold colour of these ribbons is still apparent in this piece. It is easy to see why so many women saved the ribbons in order to create such sumptuous designs from them. Yellow was the most common colour for the silk ribbons; other colours such as blue, red and pink were also used. The different colours of ribbons denoted the different grades of cigars that were bound by them.

Despite these pieces being made from common ribbons – essentially a pretty way of recycling – few of these quilts have survived. Many of the ribbons were low-quality silk and simply disintegrated with age. This quilt top is not only still intact but has also retained its rich colour. Silk cigar ribbon quilts of this quality are extremely rare.

LEFT: Close-up details of company names on the cigar ribbons.

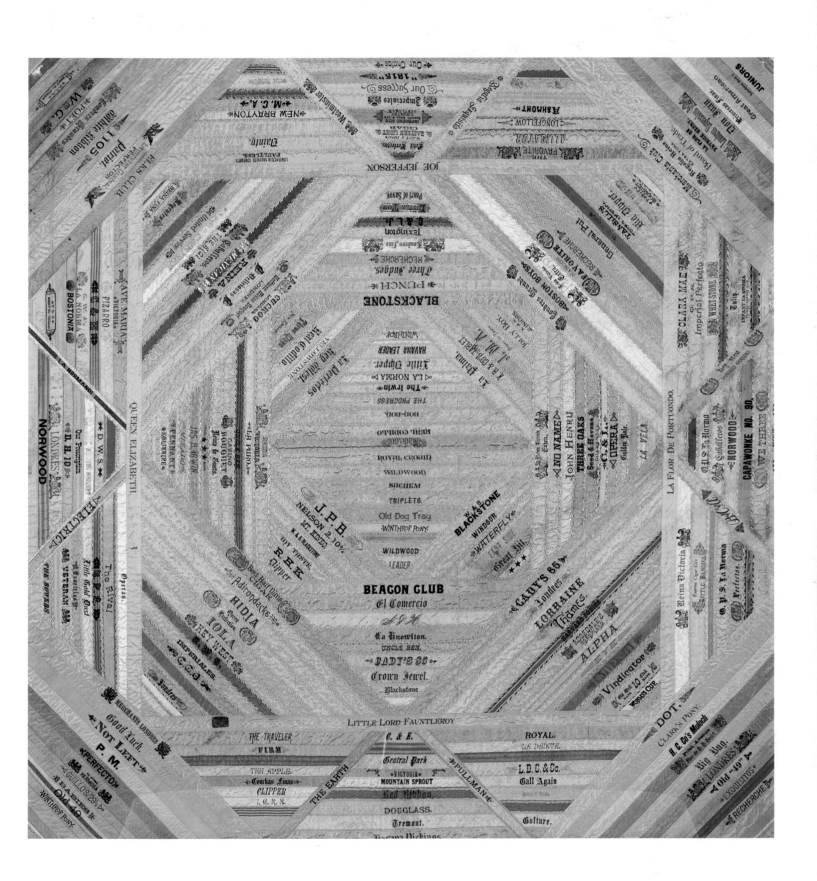

Square-in-a-Square Quilt

1835–50
Philadelphia, Pennsylvania
Quaker
244 x 213 cm (96 x 84 in)
1960.813

Forty-two Square-in-a-Square blocks, joined together with striped fabric. The quilt is made from silk in subtle shades of fawn, brown, blue and gold. The squares are quilted with cross-hatching and straight parallel lines, the sashing with a leaf motif. Backed with bright blue glazed cotton.

It is a common misconception that Quaker quilts are plain and (by implication) dull. Most are kaleidoscopes of expensive silks and bright cottons. This quilt is no exception, using luminous silks (some of which are delicately patterned) to create an attractive geometric design that showcases the fine fabrics used.

The quilt belonged to the Yarnall family who were prominent Quakers living in Pennsylvania. Many eminent families employed a sewing woman, who regularly visited the house to make new clothes (or other textiles) required by the family and to repair damaged items. It is believed that this quilt was made by the Yarnall family's sewing woman from pieces of silk left over from her dressmaking tasks.

Some of the triangles in the blocks have been pieced together from smaller scraps of fabric. It is likely that the material used for the sashing between each block was not a dressmaking remnant but was bought to make the quilt. The same blue, yellow and black striped silk has been used for all the sashing and the lines of the silk run parallel to the blocks. It is doubtful whether this effect would have been achieved with fabric scraps. Similarly, the glazed blue cotton used for the backing was probably bought for the quilt. This cotton was often used by Quakers for quilt backing and is the same as that used on another Quaker quilt in the collection, the following Tumbling Blocks Star (see pp.104–5).

ABOVE: The sashing fabric has been carefully cut to ensure that the design lines run parallel to the blocks.

Tumbling Blocks Star Quilt

*c.*1852
Crosswicks, New Jersey
Made by Dr Sarah Taylor Middleton Rogers
255 x 255 cm (103 x 103 in)
1962.91

Very large show quilt of silk Tumbling Blocks sewn together in a star formation. The entire Tumbling Blocks design is appliquéd onto a background of blue striped silk. Backed with bright blue glazed cotton. Hand-quilted with scallops, oak leaf designs and parallel lines (¼ in apart).

This magnificent quilt was made by a Quaker for exhibition at the New Jersey State Fair, held in Trenton in 1852. Each Tumbling Block is

made from three pieces of silk (of light, medium and dark shades) that have been tacked onto diamond shaped papers and then sewn together. The individual blocks have been arranged to form an eye-dazzling twelve-pointed star that creates optical illusions. Not surprisingly, the maker of this quilt won an award: a silver ladle inscribed 'Premium to S.T.M. For Silk Quilt 10 Mo. 1852'.

Although the blocks and the quilting have been sewn by hand, the background fabric of blue striped silk has been assembled from three lengths of fabric stitched together by a sewing machine. In 1852, treadle sewing machines were still expensive novelties. Sarah Taylor Middleton (later Mrs Rogers) was one of the earliest female

physicians in Pennsylvania and, as such, probably had sufficient money to spend on this curious innovation.

Sarah was an exceptional needlewoman, who recognized that success depended on attention to detail. The striped background fabric has been joined to make it large enough to contain the substantial Tumbling Blocks design. Each pinstripe has been precisely aligned to ensure continuity in the printed pattern. The hand-quilting is meticulous. Simple parallel lines cover most of the quilt top. Scallop filler is used in the borders and quilted oak leaves are stitched between the star points.

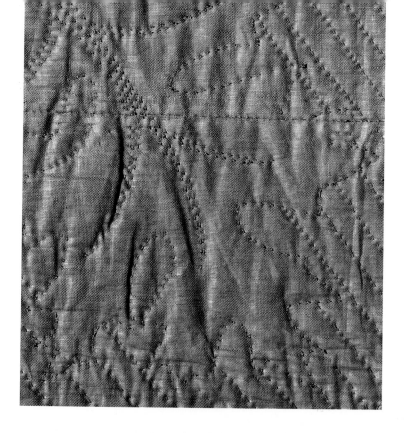

LEFT: Glazed blue cotton was commonly used by Quakers as quilt backing. The same material that backs this quilt is also used on Square-in-a-Square Quilt, the other Quaker quilt in the museum's collection (see pp.102–3).

ABOVE: Care has been taken to align the tiny stripes when joining pieces of the background fabric.

BELOW: Diamonds of fabric form the strong geometric pattern of Tumbling Blocks.

ABOVE: Shoo Fly blocks,
set on point, alternate
with elaborately quilted
plain blocks.

LEFT: The block in the
top right-hand corner is
odd, with grey triangles
instead of black.

Shoo Fly Quilt

1929
Milton, Iowa
Amish
218 x 184 cm (86 x 72 in)
1980.67

*Set on point, twenty Shoo Fly blocks (10 in square)
alternate with plain black squares. Patterned blocks
(four across, five down) pieced from plain black
cotton and brown wool; the top and bottom row
blocks use beige wool instead of brown. The blocks
are framed by a light brown inner border (2 in
wide) and a black outer border (5 in wide). Bound
with glazed black cotton and hand-quilted.*

Collectively known as the 'Plain People', the
Amish abide by the *Ordnung*, a set of rules
that applies to all Amish communities, stipulating

what is and is not acceptable in terms of dress and decoration. There is a further (unwritten) code of behaviour particular to each church. These secondary regulations (which depend on the strictness of individual communities) have the largest impact on quilt-making by determining what colours and patterns are acceptable.

Although there are many Amish settlements throughout America and Canada – often consisting of only one church district – the major Amish settlements are in Pennsylvania, Ohio and Indiana. The Shoo Fly quilt is one of the most popular patterns among Amish communities in Iowa (along with Nine-Patch and Bow Tie). This example is a typical arrangement of these blocks (set on point and alternated with plain blocks). As here, the blocks are often surrounded by an inner border and a wider outer border. This quilt uses both wool and cotton – the latter had begun to replace wool in quilts by the twentieth century.

The blocks in the top and bottom row have a beige, rather than brown, background. One block has grey triangles, while all the others have black. Many quilts feature odd blocks in an otherwise uniform design. Did the quilter, believing only God to be perfect, include a deliberate mistake?

RIGHT: Plain cream backing shows the neatness of the black quilting stitches.

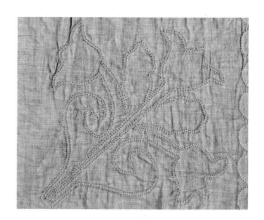

LEFT: Wide borders and binding are typical of quilts made by Amish communities in Pennsylvania.

RIGHT: Quilted tulips show a Pennsylvania-Deutsch (Dutch) influence. This detail is particularly clear on the woollen backing.

Bars Quilt

*c.*1880
Lancaster County, Pennsylvania
Amish
201 x 178 cm (79 x 70 in)
1977.93

Five brown bars alternate with four maroon bars inside a tan border (the same tan wool used for the binding), surrounded by an outer maroon border with brown squares in the corner. Backed with natural coloured wool. The central medallion is covered with diamond quilting, while scrolling feather vines are quilted in the outer border, with tulips in the corner blocks.

Amish communities were slower than their neighbours to adopt quilt-making. As a consequence, most surviving Amish quilts were made after 1880. Earlier quilts do exist but are very rare. Interestingly – and seemingly at odds with their general resistance to technological innovations – the Amish were quick to adopt the sewing machine for piecing quilts. Treadle machines became an integral part of any Amish home.

Late nineteenth-century Amish quilts have simple designs, usually Diamond-in-a-Square, Centre Square or Bars. These early quilts were made from factory-produced fine wool or cotton; occasionally, homespun was used. This example uses a natural colour scheme of brown, tan and red. Such sombre schemes are typical of Amish quilts of this period.

Amish quilts are valued for their fine quilting and those from Lancaster County are executed with great skill. As this is an early Amish quilt, the quilting is still fairly plain, with diamond filler covering the centre. Early Amish quilts usually have brown quilting thread, as in this example. Another indication of an early quilt is the use of double-stitched lines: here, the corner tulip designs – a Pennsylvania-Deutsch ('Dutch') influence – have been stitched in this way.

Diamond-in-a-Square Quilt

1920–30
Lancaster County, Pennsylvania
Amish
193 x 193 cm (76 x 76 in)
1997.102

Woollen maroon red square, set on point in a grey square, surrounded by a maroon border (4 in wide), with grey corner blocks (4 in square). Outer border of purple wool, with grey corner blocks (13 in wide). Bound in red fabric used for the centre square and backed with plain green cotton. Feather wreath quilted in central square, surrounded by cross-hatching. Scrolling feather vine is used in the outer border.

Lancaster County in Pennsylvania is the site of the oldest continuously occupied Amish community in the United States. It is also considered one of the most relaxed in terms of 'acceptable' quilt designs. Lancaster County quilts are distinctly different from other Amish communities in America. The most popular designs in Lancaster County are: Diamond-in-a-Square, Bars, Sunshine and Shadow, Grandmother's Dream, Double Nine-Patch, Nine-Patch Variations, Centre Square and Baskets.

This pattern is virtually unique to Lancaster County and one of the first to be adopted by them. It uses the medallion style of quilt-making, with a large central design surrounded by a wide border – a style considered outdated in the early twentieth century by non-Amish quilters. Once a quilt design was deemed old-fashioned in the wider world, it was considered an acceptable design by the Amish.

Quilts made in Lancaster County are typically square, with wide borders and binding. The outer border usually measures between ten and fifteen inches in width. The binding on this example (an inch wide) is typical of quilts from this area. Wool was commonly used for these quilts until the 1940s, when cheaper synthetic materials began to be used.

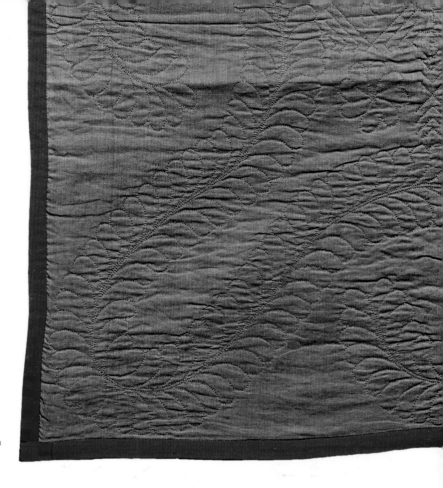

RIGHT: The quilting is as fine on the back as it is on the front.

ABOVE: A variety of quilting patterns adorns the quilt.

LEFT: Grey alpaca wool backing.

Floating Bars Quilt

*c.*1900
Ohio
Amish
244 x 191 cm (88 x 75 in)
1977.2

*Three forest green and four maroon bars (each
7½ in wide) alternate within a lavender border
(4½ in wide). Black glazed cotton outer border
(3½ in wide). Backed with grey alpaca that has been
turned over onto the front to bind the quilt. Cable
quilting in the green bars, diamond quilting in the
maroon bars. Flowers and leaves have been quilted
in the lavender border and ovals in the outer border.*

The Amish communities in east central Ohio
constitute the largest concentration of Amish
living anywhere in the world. There are Amish
communities in Holmes County, Wayne County,
Stark County and Tuscarawas County. Although
adhering to the conventions of Amish quilt-
making – keeping design and colour simple – there
are several key differences between quilts made in
Ohio and those made in Lancaster County.

The Ohio Amish use a much wider variety of
patterns than their Lancaster County counterparts.
While the Lancaster County Amish prefer simple
medallion-style quilts, many Ohio Amish quilts
are made from more elaborately pieced tops. Some
quilts even have pieced backs. The use of decorated
fabric is also permitted in this community
(provided the pattern is fairly inconspicuous).

As this is an early Ohio Amish quilt, the
arrangement is uncomplicated. The design is a
variation of Bars but, unlike the similar example
from Lancaster County (see p.108), this particular
quilt does not have corner blocks in a wide border.
Instead, it has two narrower borders – hence the
slight change in design name to Floating Bars.
Unusually, this quilt has glazed black cotton for
the outer border. Black was not a popular colour
choice until after the First World War and lost its
popularity by the 1940s.

ABOVE: Rose of Sharon is one of the designs alternating with the repeated Maple Leaf block.

Garden Wreath Quilt

1840–1900
Possibly Pennsylvania
221 x 180 cm (87 x 71 in)
1962.16

Twelve appliqué blocks (with floral designs) on white background alternate with yellow blocks (with green pieced Maple Leaf design). The blocks are set on point, with a wide border containing an appliqué wandering tulip design. Backing and binding are of white cotton, with thin border of red cotton.

This quilt alternates repeated Maple Leaf blocks with variously decorated and constructed floral blocks. Although not itself a sampler quilt, this example is similar in that all its floral blocks are different; some are pieced, some appliquéd. Variations of the Rose Wreath, Rose of Sharon and Lily blocks are featured. These apparently disparate parts are unified by a limited colour palette (red, green, white and yellow) and the rhythmic placement of the repeated blocks. The colours of the quilt and the inclusion of a wandering tulip border suggest that this quilt may have been made in Pennsylvania. Tulips often figure in the decorative arts of the Pennsylvania-Deutsch ('Dutch').

The blocks that are pieced have been done by machine; the quilting, however, is by hand. All of the block designs and the wandering tulip border have been outline-quilted. The Maple Leaf blocks have been filled with straight parallel lines, while the floral blocks have scallop filler in the white areas. The border is quilted with running feather vines on either side of the appliqué design; scallop quilting embellishes the remaining border areas.

The binding of this quilt is of particular interest. The plain white backing has been folded to the front and hand-stitched in place to form the binding. Before being secured, a thin strip of folded red cotton has been inserted under the seam and stitched together under the seam of the binding. This has created a thin 'pipe' between the wider appliqué border and the binding.

Princess Feather Quilt

1850–1900
Pennsylvania
201 x 201 cm (79 x 79 in)
1960.308

Four red and green Princess Feather designs appliquéd onto a white background. Eight pairs of red and green feathers have been applied to form a border. Finely quilted with feather wreaths and diamond filler. Bound with plain red fabric.

The feather motif is an old and popular quilting motif from the north of England. The convention of including feather motifs in quilts was brought to America when English settlers sought out a new life for themselves in the Colonies. The progression from quilting design to appliqué is a natural one and applied feather designs can be found on quilts dating from the beginning of the nineteenth century to the present day.

As well as traditional English quilting patterns, other possible sources of inspiration for the design include the exaggerated European depictions of high-born Native American women (or 'princesses') wearing elaborate headdresses. Princess Feather could also be a corruption of 'the Prince's feathers' – the heraldic badge of the Prince of Wales. Moreover, when ladies were presented at court, etiquette dictated that they wore plumes in their hair.

This quilt has been skilfully assembled. By splitting each feather in half with green and red fabric, a spinning motion is created. The white areas of the quilt have been covered with intricate patterns. The feathers themselves are accentuated with outline quilting, while feather wreaths – with diamond filler – are quilted in the large areas. Straight parallel lines define the border and the remaining areas are filled with diamond quilting.

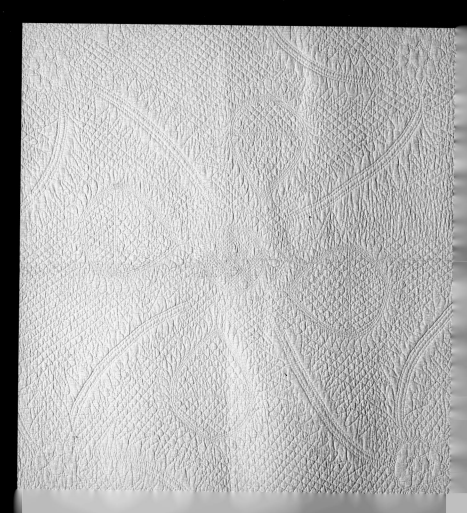

RIGHT: The swirling motion of the feathers on the front (above) is picked out by the quilting, shown here on the back (below).

ABOVE: Queen Kapi'olani on a
cabinet card, c.1880 (1980.85.2).

LEFT: Thick wadding enhances
the contour quilting.

BELOW: Star, Dart and Feather
quilts – such as this example
made in Pennsylvania during
the early nineteenth century
(1959.37) – are stylistically
similar to Hawaiian quilts.

Queen Kapi'olani's Fan Quilt

Early twentieth century
Hawaii
191 x 221 cm (75 x 83 in)
1972.157

Single-piece appliqué feather and fan design in red on white background with floral appliqué border. Close contour hand-quilting (1½ in apart) and thick wadding give the surface of the quilt a three-dimensional quality. Plain white backing and plain red binding.

Traditionally, Hawaiians used *kapa* cloths (made from beaten mulberry bark) as bedcovers – the climate on the islands being too warm for thick multilayered quilts. It is thought that missionaries introduced Hawaiian women to the art of quilting as a suitable alternative to forbidden dances and ceremonies. Quilting was embraced by the women, who produced pieces that were distinctly Hawaiian in design.

This example, with its striking contrast between dark appliquéd design and light background, is typical of Hawaiian quilts. The central pattern has been cut from a large piece of fabric, folded and cut to produce a symmetrical motif. This design is reminiscent of feather quilts, popular among the Pennsylvania-Deutsch ('Dutch').

The stylized feather and fan design is a traditional Hawaiian pattern. Like the Hawaiian flag quilts (see pp.118–19), it has a sentimental meaning. The fans represent the fan of Queen Consort Kapi'olani (1834–1899). The feathers refer to the royal coat of arms, which is supported by a pair of warrior chiefs holding *kahilis* (feather plume standards). The border of the quilt is an appliqué *Maile lei* design, a traditional Hawaiian flower garland.

Ku'u Hae Aloha Quilt

*c.*1893
Hawaii
203 x 178 cm (80 x 70 in)
1972.161

Central panel (39 x 30 in) with the coronet and shield of the Hawaiian royal coat of arms appliquéd onto white background. Appliqué design is herringbone-stitched with yellow thread. Central panel surrounded by four machine-pieced Hawaiian flags. Bound with red cotton and backed with white cotton of two pieces. Contour quilting enhances the appliqué design.

Of all Hawaiian quilts, those most treasured are the ones that feature the Hawaiian flag. It is unusual for these quilts to leave the family of the quilt-maker because they are so highly prized. Featuring the Hawaiian flag and royal coat of arms, they were made to honour and commemorate the Hawaiian kingdom and its period of independence for most of the nineteenth century. These quilts also pay homage to the Hawaiian kings and queens.

For twenty-two years, the Union Jack was used as the flag of the Hawaiian kingdom. After 1816, this emblem was incorporated into the design of the new flag – a token of the many years Hawaii was under British protection. It was originally believed that these related quilts were made as a reaction against the forced abdication of the queen of Hawaii in 1893. Subsequent research has suggested, however, that these flag quilts were first constructed as early as 1843 – the year in which a serious attempt was made to overthrow the Hawaiian government.

The design of these flag quilts varies and thus can give some indication as to when they were made. The earliest quilts have only seven stripes on the Hawaiian flag. Each of the stripes represents one of the principal inhabited islands of Hawaii. In 1870, Kauai became part of Hawaii – previously it had been a tributary kingdom – and so another stripe was added to the flag. After 1883, the coat of arms became more ornate (with a crown suspended over a draped cape and with a *formée* cross beneath). Many feature the slogan *Ku'u Hae Aloha*, which translates as 'My Beloved Flag'.

RIGHT: Hawaiian royal coat of arms adorns the centre of the quilt.

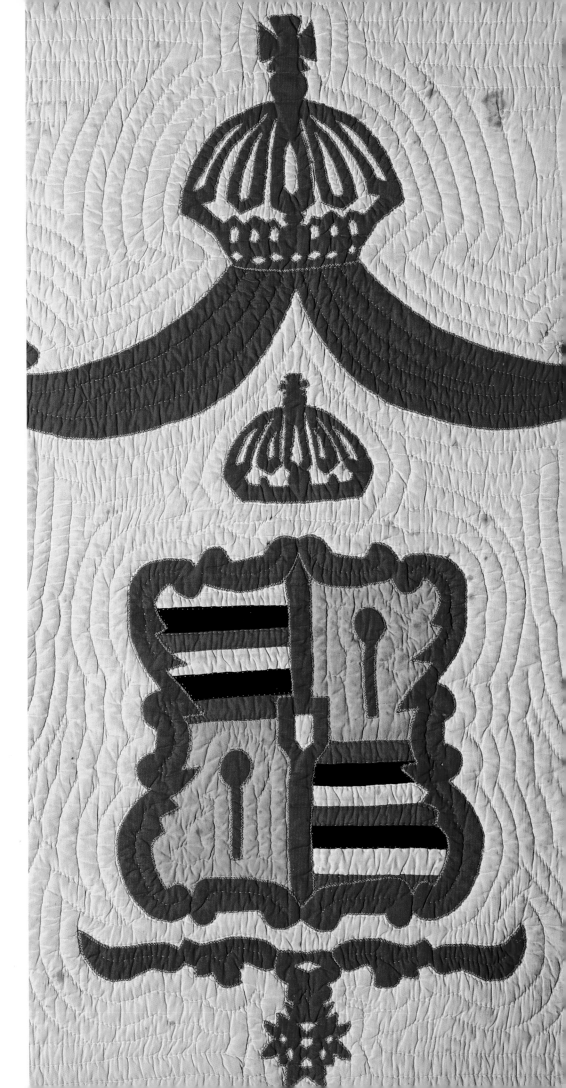

Trip Around the World Quilt

1930s
America
198 x 191 cm (78 x 75 in)
1992.154

One-inch squares, set on point, arranged in bands to form Trip Around the World pattern. Squares cut from multicoloured patterned cottons and machine-pieced. Filled with light wadding and backed with green cotton. Each square has been hand-quilted a quarter of an inch from its edge. Bound with cream cotton.

Each tiny square has been machine-pieced together to ensure that the colours run in regimented lines. This quilt showcases the delicately printed cottons available in the early decades of the twentieth century. The finesse of this quilt – decorated with simple outline quilting – is the precision piecing of these brightly coloured fabrics.

This quilt was made by an unknown quilter and given to Eleanor Roosevelt, the wife of Franklin D. Roosevelt (thirty-second President of the United States). The gift was an appropriate one for Mrs Roosevelt, who used her influence to spearhead craft training projects under the Works Progress Administration during the Depression. The aim of the project was to encourage Americans to re-learn traditional craft skills, including quilt-making (in which there was a resurgence of interest during this time of thriftiness).

In 1941 – the year the United States entered the Second World War, after the bombing of the Pearl Harbor naval base in Hawaii – Eleanor Roosevelt gave this quilt to her eldest grandson, who used it on his bed. Nicknamed 'Buzzy' by the press, President Roosevelt's grandson lived in the White House for several years. Buzzy and his sister (nicknamed 'Sistie') were well known to the public as they were often in attendance at the President's breakfast meetings, where he would play with them between reviewing policies. They were known as 'the first grandchildren'.

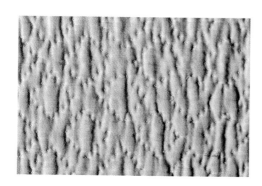

LEFT: Heavy quilting outlines each tiny square.

ABOVE: Small squares have been meticulously pieced.

Red Cross Quilt

*c.*1944
Canada
180 x 140 cm (71 x 55 in)
2000.10

Quilt top pieced from large squares and rectangles of fabric sewn together in geometric design. The fabric was probably cut from discarded blue, grey and brown suits. Hand-quilted with straight parallel lines running diagonally across the quilt. Backed with blue, red and white striped fabric.

During the Second World War, the American and Canadian Red Cross Societies organized shipments of quilts to Europe for soldiers and dispossessed people. The Red Cross provided backing and batting to community groups, which used these materials to assemble quilts. Individual groups kept a record of how many quilts they gave to the Red Cross. One district alone sent over three thousand. Unfortunately, there are no records of the total number of American and Canadian quilts sent to Europe during the war.

This quilt top has been assembled from large blocks of dark woollen suit fabric. Wool was often used for the amount of warmth it would provide. The quilting is uncomplicated and thus allowed for rapid completion. The blue and red striped flannelette used for the backing appears on many Red Cross quilts and was probably a standard fabric issued by them to volunteer quilt-makers. The backing has been turned and stitched to the front of the quilt for the binding.

This quilt was sent over by the Canadian Red Cross Society. The Red Cross labels that were originally attached to the back of the quilt have been removed. A woman, whose home in Surrey had been bombed in 1944, received the quilt. It is in excellent condition – unusual for a Red Cross example – because the recipient never used the quilt, fearing that this unexpected gift would get damaged if she did so.

LEFT: The striped backing fabric is typical of many Red Cross quilts and may have been supplied by the organization to quilt groups.

Lady in the White House Quilt

1939–45
Wheatley, Canada
206 x 167 cm (81 x 66 in)
1998.123

Twenty blocks (13½ in wide) machine-pieced from scraps of fabric. The blocks are separated by sashing (2½ in wide) made of green fabric with white polka dots. Backed with plain green flannelette that has also been used for the binding. Hand-quilted with straight parallel lines that run diagonally across the quilt.

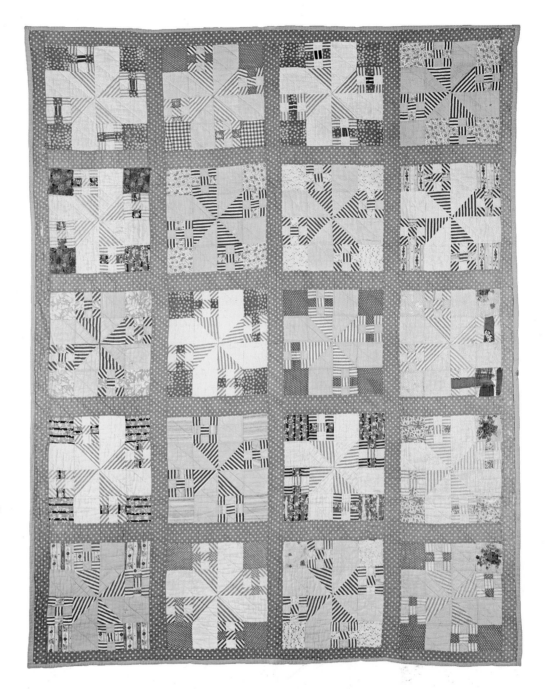

The blocks in this quilt top have been machine-pieced together from squares and triangles. Each block uses three different fabrics. The backing has been machine-pieced from green flannelette that was used in American quilts of this period. It has been turned to the front to form the binding and machine-stitched in place. The hand-quilting is a simple design to enable speed in completing this quilt. On the back is a fabric label with a red cross, which reads: 'Canadian Red Cross Society, Wheatley Branch'.

Unlike knitted 'Bundles for Britain' items, relief quilts had no prescribed pattern. Many of the quilts produced were of a Crazy design, using large scraps of material (usually wool or suit fabric). This enabled the maker to construct a quilt top in a short amount of time. Similarly, quilting was often discarded in favour of the quicker method of tying the layers together. In their eagerness to get quilts to those who needed them as quickly as possible, many quilters pulled out old quilt tops that had never been completed. It was a short task to layer them up and quilt them. As this example uses a block pattern, rather than the more common scrap design, it is possible that this was one such quilt top.

This particular quilt was sent to Lincolnshire for use by evacuees. After the war ended, no other organization would accept the quilts and so they were distributed among local people. The quilt was passed on to a grateful bride, who had a farmhouse to furnish with only enough coupons in her ration book for a few sheets and blankets.

RIGHT: Red Cross quilts were more typically of a Crazy design, like this Canadian example (2003.29) from 1939–40.

One-Patch Quilt – Diamonds Variation

*c.*1969
Gee's Bend, Alabama
242 x 195 cm (95 x 77 in)
2003.9

Set on point, alternating squares of green and fuchsia velveteen are framed by a fuchsia border. A contrasting brown colour has been used for corner triangles and in eight central squares. Machine-pieced and hand-quilted in white thread. The quilting is of freehand parallel lines, approximately one inch apart. Straight lines intersect the diagonal parallel lines at random intervals, often ending abruptly. The quilt is backed with cream cotton, which has been turned over to the front to create the binding.

The African-American rural community at Gee's Bend, Alabama, numbers about seven hundred. The geographic isolation of Gee's Bend has resulted in the community often experiencing a delay in receiving modern innovations. New housing and other amenities were provided for the community under Franklin D. Roosevelt's New Deal programmes in the 1930s.

As part of his work to document Civil Rights abuses, the Episcopal priest Francis X. Walter was in Alabama during the 1960s. He saw the quilts being produced by the women of Gee's Bend and recognized the opportunity to form a co-operative business, making these quilts for sale.

On 26 March 1966, the quilters met in a local Baptist church and established the Freedom Quilting Bee. This was the first business owned by African-Americans in Wilcox County, Alabama. The quilts were sold in New York City, and the cheque for the first seventy quilts sold ($2,065) was spent on necessities such as washing machines, indoor plumbing and the tuition payment needed to send the great-granddaughter of a slave to college.

The Gee's Bend quilts were incredibly popular. Soon large companies wanted to stock them in their stores. In June 1969, sales of the quilts – including this one – began in Bloomingdale's. These large companies demanded a level of consistency in their products and supplied the Freedom Quilting Bee with new materials, ranging from synthetics to Liberty cottons. Working in conjunction with Bloomingdale's, a designer was employed to produce new patterns (some of them based on abstract designs). Many of the quilters felt these new production regulations curbed their creativity. The demand for their quilts was short-lived; the contract with Bloomingdale's ended within a few years. Although no longer a great commercial success, the ladies of Gee's Bend continued quilting. Their pieces are now celebrated as great works of art and have been displayed in major museums in the United States.

LEFT: Quilted straight lines intersect at seemingly random intervals.

RIGHT: The batting has worn away in places, so that the velveteen on the quilt front is visible through the backing fabric.

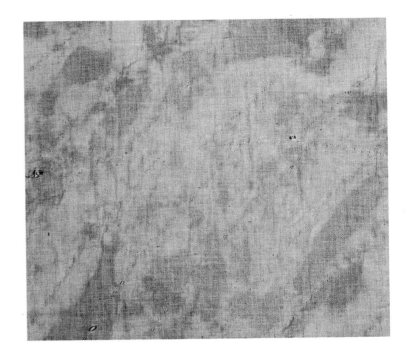

Glossary

Appliqué: The technique of applying fabric shapes on top of a backing fabric. The edges are turned under, and the piece is stitched into place, sometimes with decorative embroidery stitches.

Backing: The fabric on the back of the quilt. It is usually only one fabric but can sometimes be as elaborately pieced as the quilt top.

Batting: The layer between the quilt top and the backing. Batting provides the thickness and warmth in a quilt. Cotton and wool were commonly used for batting, but anything would do: some quilts have old blankets as the middle layer.

Binding: A thin strip of fabric sewn around the edge of a quilt to enclose the raw edges formed by the backing, batting and top.

Block: A basic unit of quilt construction, usually in the form of a square, which is repeated or arranged in rows to form the design of a quilt top.

Contour quilting: Quilting that echoes the line of the patchwork design and radiates out to the edge of the quilt.

Cording: The insertion of thick cord (often candlewick) between stitches sewn onto the quilt top, in order to create a raised line.

Foundation piecing: Pieces of fabric sewn onto a temporary or permanent piece of foundation fabric (or paper). This method is often used to make Log Cabin and Crazy blocks.

In-the-ditch quilting: Quilting stitches that run along the seams of the patchwork design. For quilting that has a gap between the seams and stitches see *Outline quilting*.

Knife-edge binding: A method of enclosing the raw edges of a quilt where the sides of the top and backing are folded in towards each other and sewn together.

Medallion quilt: A quilt that has a large central design motif that is surrounded by one or more borders.

Nine-Patch: A patchwork block made up of nine squares, arranged in a three-by-three formation to make a larger square. This is a common patchwork block and forms the foundation for many more elaborate designs.

On point: The placing of a square block so that it sits diagonally in a quilt, with the corners (or points) aligned with the straight edges of the quilt.

Outline quilting: Quilt stitches that follow a patchwork or appliqué design. The stitches usually have a small border between them and the edge of the design. For quilting that runs along the seam see *In-the-ditch quilting*.

Paper piecing: Fabric pieces applied to paper templates before being sewn together to form a pattern. This method is often used for hexagon and diamond arrangements.

Patchwork: A design pieced together from fabric, often used to make a quilt top.

Pieced: The assembly of fabric shapes that have been cut and sewn together. The seams are hidden on the reverse of the quilt top, and there is no foundation fabric.

Quilt: A bedcover usually made of three layers (quilt top, batting and backing) sewn or tied together.

Quilting: Decorative stitches used to hold layers of a quilt together.

Reverse appliqué: The creation of design shapes by cutting away the top layer of fabric to expose the fabric beneath it.

Sashing: Lengths of fabric that divide and join blocks of patchwork on a quilt top.

Stuffed: The insertion of stuffing or yarn between layers of a quilt to give height/texture to a specific area.

Tied: A quick method of holding the layers of a quilt together: instead of quilting, thread is passed through the layers and tied.

Trapunto: Stuffing inserted through backing.

Wadding: See *Batting*.

Whole-Cloth: A bedcover or quilt in which the top is made from lengths of the same fabric.

Bibliography

The American Museum in Britain

America in Britain. Annual journal published by The American Museum in Britain.

Barghini, Sandra. *Aspects of America: The American Museum in Britain* (London: Scala Publishers, 2007)

Chapman, Dick. *Dallas Pratt: A Patchwork Biography* (Cambridge: Mark Argent, 2004)

Chapman, Dick. *Four Men and a Fortune* (Cambridge: Mark Argent, 2005)

Garrett, Wendell (ed.). *The Magazine Antiques* (March 1993) [The American Museum in Britain special issue]

American Quilts and their History

Beardsley, John, *et al. The Quilts of Gee's Bend* (Atlanta, Georgia: Tinwood Books, in association with the Museum of Fine Arts, Houston, 2002)

Betterton, Shiela. *Quilts and Coverlets from The American Museum in Britain* (Frome and London: Butler and Tanner Ltd, in association with The American Museum in Britain, 1978)

Betterton, Shiela. *More Quilts and Coverlets from The American Museum in Britain* (Frome and London: Butler and Tanner Ltd, in association with The American Museum in Britain, 1989)

Brackman, Barbara. *Clues in the Calico: A Guide to Identifying and Dating Antique Quilts* (Charlottesville, Virginia: Howell Press, 1989)

Brackman, Barbara. *Facts and Fabrications: Unraveling the History of Quilts and Slavery* (Lafayette, California: C. and T. Publishing, 2006)

Brick, Cindy. *Crazy Quilts: History, Techniques, Embroidery Motifs* (Minnesota: Voyageur Press, 2008)

Colby, Averil. *Quilting* (London: B. T. Batsford Ltd, 1972)

Granick, Eve Wheatcroft. *The Amish Quilt* (Intercourse, Pennsylvania: Good Books, 1989)

Horton, Laurel, *et al. Quiltmaking in America: Beyond the Myths* (Nashville, Tennessee: Rutledge Hill Press, 1994)

Katzenberg, Dena S. *Baltimore Album Quilts* (Baltimore, Maryland: Baltimore Museum of Art, 1981)

Keller, Patricia J. '*Of the Best Sort but Plain': Quaker Quilts from the Delaware Valley, 1760–1890* (Chadds Ford, Pennsylvania: Brandywine River Museum, 1996)

Kirakofe, Roderick, and Johnson, Mary Elizabeth. *The American Quilt: A History of Cloth and Comfort, 1750–1950* (New York: Clarkson Potter, Inc., 1993)

Orlofsky, Patsy and Myron. *Quilts in America* (New York: McGraw-Hill Book Company, 1974)

Robare, Mary Holton. 'Mosaic Autograph Friendship Quilt, Dated 1848: Research Notes-in-progress' (November 2008), The American Museum in Britain archives

Roberts, Elise Schebler. *The Quilt: A History and Celebration of an American Art Form* (Minnesota: Voyageur Press, 2007)

Safford, Carleton L., and Bishop, Robert. *America's Quilts and Coverlets* (New York: E. P. Dutton & Co., Inc., 1972)

Shaw, Robert. *Hawaiian Quilt Masterpieces* (Southport, Connecticut: Hugh Lauter Levin Associates, Inc., 1996)

Websites

Iowa–Illinois Quilt Study Group, 2 April 2005 meeting. See www.quilthistory.com/study/apr2.htm

Whaley, John Corey, and Roach, Susan. 'Maggie Skipwith Smith (12/12/1874–2/16/1957): "Our George's Cherry Tree" Quilt'. See www.louisianafolklife.org/quilts/features/cherry_tree.shtm

Wulfert, Kimberley. 'Patriotic Quilts through Time'. See www.antiquequiltdating.com/Patriotic_Quilts_Through_Time.html

Index

Note: Page numbers in *italics* are for illustrations

ABOVE: Bridal Chest Quilt, detail (see pp.32–3).

© Scala Publishers Ltd, 2009
Text © The American Museum in Britain, 2009
Photography © The American Museum in Britain, 2009

First published in 2009 by
Scala Publishers Ltd
Northburgh House
10 Northburgh St
London EC1V 0AT
Telephone: +44 (0) 20 7490 9900
www.scalapublishers.com
ISBN-13: 978 1 85759 598 7

Furthermore: a Program of the J.M. Kaplan Fund
awarded a generous grant towards the publication of
this book.

Text: Laura Beresford and Katherine Hebert
Editor (Scala): Matthew Taylor
Project Editor (Scala): Esme West
Design: Yvonne Dedman
Printed and bound in Italy
10 9 8 7 6 5 4 3 2 1

Acknowledgements

This book has been a collaborative effort, and
its success is very much due to the splendid quilt
photography by Daniel Brown. Daniel spent
much of his time balanced precariously on
ladders to achieve the best viewpoint and
adjusting lights to showcase these quilts to best
advantage. We cannot thank him enough.

The authors would also like to take this
opportunity to thank the following individuals
and organizations for making this publication
possible: Sandra Barghini, Director, and the
Trustees and Councils of The American Museum
in Britain; Susan Anne Mathisen and the staff
of the Halcyon Foundation (a New York based
organization for the supporters of the American
Museum living in the United States) and the staff
at Scala Publishers.

We were delighted with the support we received
from fellow quilt enthusiasts, who were always
quick to respond to our queries as we prepared
this book. We extend tremendous thanks to the
following: Madge Ziegler of Newark, Delaware,
who sent details and scans of the Eagle Appliqué
Quilt kit mentioned on page 70; quilt historian
Kimberly Wulfert, who also provided additional
information about this particular example
(1998.156); and Mary Holton Robare, who
unstintingly spent so much of her time
researching the identities behind the names on
the Mosaic Friendship Quilt from Shepherdstown,
West Virginia (2008.1), featured on pages 52–3.

This publication would not have been as
successful without the support of our colleagues
at The American Museum in Britain, notably
Judi Grant, who prepared the many quilts for
photography, and Stuart Ross, who supplied
additional images (and regular chocolate). We
must also thank the people and pets who share
our homes. They did not see much of us during
the time we were chained to our computers.

Finally, we would like to express our immense
gratitude to the many people who have gifted
quilts to The American Museum in Britain.
Thanks to these generous donations – too
numerous to be included in this publication – the
wonderful quilts in the museum's collection will
continue to be enjoyed and admired by future
generations.